Kundalini and the Chakras

Open Your Third Eye Through Self-Healing Techniques and Learn How to Balance and Unblock Your Chakras

Laura Connelly

TABLE OF CONTENTS

INTRODUCTION

Congratulations on purchasing *Kundalini and the Chakras,* and thank you for doing so.

The following chapters will discuss the incredible journey you are about to embark on as you begin to learn the knowledge that you need to know about the Kundalini and how to awaken it inside of you. You will soon see where the Kundalini comes from and what it feels like when yours begins to awaken. You will learn how to balance your Kundalini as it begins to stimulate and how you can support it while you are developing your Kundalini.

You are about to begin a journey that will change your life. With your Kundalini in action, your life will be nothing like it was before. You will discover a power inside of you that you never knew existed, and that power can transform your life, once you have learned what it is and what to do with it.

Kundalini is a potential force that lives inside of everyone, a dormant yet powerful force waiting to be awakened and utilized. This energy from the divine will be the strongest when you are spiritual and energetic, and these are things that are possible when you awaken your Kundalini.

There are plenty of books on this subject on the market; thanks so much again for choosing this one! Every possible effort has been made to ensure that it is full of as much useful information as possible, so please enjoy!

CHAPTER 1

What Is Kundalini

Kundalini comes from ancient India, and it is a term that identifies the awakening and arising of consciousness and an energy that is waiting coiled at the base of your spine. This power has been waiting there since you were born. It is the source of the force that drives your life. Ancient beliefs say that this power causes the formation of the baby in the mother's womb, and then it coils itself at the base of the spine of the fetus, growing as the baby grew. The power then lies at the bottom of the spine, waiting to be unlocked, awakened, and utilized until it uncoils and returns to its source when you die.

The Energy and Consciousness of Kundalini

Kundalini is an energy that you can gain when you make a meditative and focused effort. It will provide you with a state of blissful consciousness when you have awakened it. You will uncoil the Kundalini and bring it up through all of the seven internal chakras until it reaches the Crown Chakra and affects its function. When you awaken the Kundalini inside yourself, then you will know the joy of total enlightenment.

Kundalini is a spiritual and psychological energy that animates your consciousness. It lies dormant in your sleeping body, and you can arouse it through the use of many different methods to bring new states of consciousness to yourself. When you can experience the power of Kundalini, you will feel energy like none you have ever felt before.

Most people are not aware of their own conscious and psychic abilities. Some realms lay far beyond the physical world you inhabit, and you have spiritual abilities you don't yet realize. Kundalini has been a universal phenomenon for centuries. It was often written about in the teachings of the mystics living in cultures around the world, especially those in the Far East. These people knew about the power of Kundalini and have taught others how to unlock the power down through the generations.

While there is writing on how to awaken the Kundalini rapidly, it is far better to do the awakening slowly and purposefully. An explosive awakening might be too much for your system to handle. You will want to bring the Kundalini to your Crown Chakra, but this ascension should be gradual and purposeful. If you were suddenly transported to the fifth dimension of reality, you would find that it is too different from the truth that you are used to and impossible to understand. You would want to be brought home suddenly, but then you might find your dimension to be dull and boring. In the same way, you do not want to awaken your Kundalini too rapidly because you might find the sudden levels of energy and enlightenment too much for you to handle all at once. Take your awakening slowly, because getting your Kundalini ascended to your Crown Chakra is not an ultimate goal but a part of your journey.

Awakening the Kundalini gradually will give you the power to enjoy yourself and to enjoy the love you will share with others who are on the same journey. You will eventually realize that all man shares one consciousness and that the process of awakening your Kundalini will bring you to this understanding. When you have elevated your spirituality to a higher vibration, you will have a sharper perception of your oneness with the universe. When you awaken your Kundalini, it will rise through the six internal chakras until it reaches the Crown Chakra. It will awaken even more as it rises through all of the levels of the chakras. When the energized Kundalini reaches the Crown Chakra, it will produce a profound transformation of revolutionary consciousness. Your mental eye will begin to see super sensual visions. Charming sights and new worlds that are full of incredible wonders will show themselves to you. You will receive power and energy and divine knowledge in ever-increasing degrees as your Kundalini brings your chakras to life as it passes through on its way to the Crown Chakra.

Location of the Kundalini

Everyone has two distinct bodies, the subtle body and the gross body. The gross body is the one you can feel and see. It is made of your limbs, torso, head, and inner organs; it is all of the physical parts of you. Your subtle body is that part of you that thinks and reasons and feels. Your Kundalini resides in your subtle body. The subtle body is made of subtle energy, psychic centers, channels of power, and drops of essence that all work together to keep your subtle body functioning.

The Kundalini is coiled in three and one-half coils at the base of your spine. Two currents of nerves run through your spinal column, and a hollow canal runs through your spinal cord. At the bottom of the open channel in the spinal cord is the Lotus of the Kundalini. This structure is a triangular-shaped mass of matter that holds the coiled power of the Kundalini. When the Kundalini is awakened, it will rise through the six lower chakras through the passage of the hollow canal in the spinal cord. As the Kundalini rises through the chakras, it will liberate another layer of your mind, causing them to become open so that you will begin to realize the beautiful powers from the different visions.

The spinal cord is created strangely. Imagine a figure eight lying down horizontally. The two parts of the figure-eight meet in the middle, and this makes the hollow channel through which the Kundalini travels. Envision many figure eights, all laying down, one on top of the other, all the way down your back. The parts that meet in the middle area are hollow. As the Kundalini begins to uncoil and awaken, it will travel slowly upward through the channel.

Purpose of the Kundalini

The Kundalini is an intelligent force, coursing through your body energetically. When the Kundalini first begins to awaken, it begins to travel up the hollow channel in the center of the spine. When the Kundalini first begins to awaken, it can be very energetic and somewhat fierce. When you activate your energy in your body, it can quickly awaken the material you have stored in your chakras. You might feel electrical sensations running like currents up your spine as your experiences and emotions grow more intense with time. Until you learn to control the surge of energy accurately, the Kundalini might feel like a small volcano surging up your spine as it starts to awaken and move.

Kundalini, as a life force, is inexhaustible. When you begin to awaken the Kundalini inside of you, you will become sensitive to the vibrational energies it will give off. As your perception becomes more enhanced, your prevailing wisdom regarding life will begin to deepen and strengthen. When your perception is increased, you will start to enjoy a more in-depth understanding of life and your position in the universe. As you gain new knowledge of life and the experiences you have, you will also be feeding your Kundalini your energy. With all of the knowledge you are gathering comes clarity, and with this clarity comes more awakening. All of this clarity will help to build up energy in your Kundalini, and this will need to be directed toward something useful.

The energy you have gathered will be used to awaken and energize the first six internal chakras as the Kundalini travels toward the Crown Chakra. The Kundalini will always direct excess energy upward. Your system of inner chakras is just like a circuit of energy systems that are all powered with one course of electricity. This circuit of power travels up your spine using the power from the Kundalini. Your awakening Kundalini will continue to work its way up to your spine until it meets some blockage that stops its progress. It will usually find a blockage in one of the first three chakras where you hold the emotions of your family issues, deep emotions, and your ancestry and past. As the energy builds behind the blockage, it will eventually break through and release the blockage from that chakra so that the Kundalini can continue on its path. Kundalini is intelligent, and it will create its cycles of rising and falling. It will travel as far as it possibly can until it encounters a blockage it can't break through. Then the Kundalini will retreat to the Root Chakra, the chakra at the base of the spine, and it will wait there until it has built up enough energy to continue in its mission. Then it will rise up through the chakras again, going further upward each time. Eventually, the Kundalini will make a complete path to the Crown Chakra, and it will create a complete circuit.

When the energy from the Kundalini has opened the lower six chakras, it will then reach the Crown Chakra, which is its mission. When this happens, you might feel a burst of energy that will travel from your Root Chakra up your spine to your Crown Chakra. Then the Kundalini will rise out of the Crown Chakra in a process that many people find exhilarating and disorienting at the same time. You will feel numerous spiritual, mental, and physical changes all in a brief period. The Kundalini will continue to arise over and over through the central channel. Depending on the power that is needed at the moment, this rising will either feel like an intense rush or a gentle wave. Kundalini is your conscious energy that will do what you need. You might need to clean out large amounts of material from your central column with a boost of energy from your Kundalini. You might need your Kundalini to simmer in your Root chakra while it clears out all of the deep dark issues that are stored there.

Once the Kundalini reaches the Crown Chakra, you will feel a bubble of energy surrounding your Crown Chakra. This bubble will begin to expand with all of the new experiences that you will gain, and it will give you the ultimate access to all of the chakras that hover above and around your head, the chakras that are not part of any human and driven by the divine. This access will consequently allow you to open the chakras beneath your feet. You will begin to realize your humanity as you enjoy your own spiritual and physical self. You will start to see things in shades of gray and not just light and dark. Once your upper chakras, and especially your Crown Chakra, are opened, you will begin to explore your lower chakras and feel comfortable in your own emotional and primal energies and desires. You will be completely open in yourself and to yourself.

The Ultimate Life Force of the Kundalini

When your Kundalini is awakened, it becomes the basis of all that is creative within you. All significant accomplishments, such as those attributed to grace, talent, creativity, or genius. When the Kundalini is awakened, it not only inspires yogis and shamans, but it also inspires mathematicians, composers, artists, and poets. While those involved in the creative arts will be grateful for the impetus given by the Kundalini, it is the shamans and the yogis who will fully understand and completely revere the fully awakened Kundalini. They will see it as the vessel that will carry the select few followers on to the ultimate aim of all life, the goal of self-realization.

The discipline of Hatha Yoga first described the abundance of life force in the Kundalini somewhere near fifteen centuries ago. It was initially thought of as a science whose ultimate goal was to lead to the growth and ascent of the Kundalini and the power it brings to you. The ancient scriptures pointed to the necessity of meditation along with kriya (action), bandha (body strength), pranayama (breathing), and asanas (yoga) to achieve pure Kundalini awareness and spiritual enlightenment. Beyond the physical practices that are needed to awaken the Kundalini, there are also the spiritual practices of yajna (fire worship), bhakti (devotional worship), and mantra (repeated sound) to assist in awakening the Kundalini. Using the physical and spiritual practices that are dedicated to awakening the Kundalini is the most profound of all the ancient teachings.

You want to awaken your Kundalini. You want to be vibrant and alive, and totally in sync with the world around you and the larger universe. You want your spirit, body, and mind to be connected, with those around you, with the people of the world, and with the universe. With the more extensive source of energy, you will receive from an awakened Kundalini, you will be able to the infinity of yourself and your nature. The power you receive from the Kundalini is the source of your creativity and wisdom. When you begin to awaken your Kundalini, you also start to awaken the divine power that is within everyone; you will see the light of your own true consciousness.

Kundalini will provide you with spiritual benefits that you will be able to feel on the physical plane and the etheric planes of the universe. As the dominant force of your Kundalini arises, it will bring strength to your well-being and your vitality. The energy will also allow you to expand your consciousness while it enhances your capacity for personal fulfillment and ultimate joy. Kundalini is not only a highly powerful spiritual system, but it is also a therapeutic practice. It will give you transformation and awakening. Your outlook on life, along with your attitudes and moods, are all driven by the light that shines out from within you. It is the radiance that real awakening will bring to you.

Your mind is the root of all of your distress. The modern lifestyle most people follow makes it too easy to fall into negative patterns of thought that pull all of the vital energy from your heart and soul. This energy is the life force that permeates all creatures and is needed to sustain life. Negative thoughts cause blockages and dysfunction in your energy system. This negativity will lead you to feel tired and disinterested. Awakening your Kundalini will give you the tools that you need to energize your systems and command your mind and body. You will be able to live more consciously as your moods and emotions are governed more effectively. Awakening your Kundalini is the peak of your spiritual progress. It aligns your inner awareness with an awareness of the divine. When your Kundalini is adequately awakened, you will achieve the ultimate freedom.

CHAPTER 2

Awakening The Kundalini

The ultimate life force in your subtle body is the Kundalini. It is your inner fire and your creative power. Once this power is activated, it is timeless and electric, and it can be paralyzing. When you start the energy, it will flow through you in the wavy shape of the serpent to which it is compared. It curves up from the base of your spine, through your gut, past your heart, and into your head. As the energy of the Kundalini flows through this channel, it will pass through all of your chakras and give them a boost of energy to activate them. The Kundalini and the chakras are both found in your subtle body. Life will pass to the Crown Chakra at the top of your head, thus providing you with an expanded state of consciousness.

Kundalini awakening will awaken the dormant energy that resides in your subtle body. You will be able to see the world with an expanded vision. You will have a keen sense of perception that will allow you to combine numerous perspectives all at once. You will be able to understand all of your feelings correctly. You will also become a master at sensing what other people are feeling and how they see the world. This is some of the enlightenment that you will achieve through awakening your Kundalini.

The comparison of the Kundalini to a sleeping serpent comes from the story of Shakti and Shiva. In the information, a resting snake that is coiled eight times is waiting at the bottom of a great mountain to unleash its magnificent power. The Goddess Shakti wants to be with Lord Shiva. Shakti is the force behind all of creation, resting at the base of the spine as she longs to rise and be one with your consciousness at the heights of your spiritual bliss. Shiva is the consciousness of the unmovable power. As Shakti dances for Shiva, he spends significant amounts of time ignoring her, waiting for that moment when he is sure that her desire to be with him is real. Only then will he join her dance, and all of creation will unfold as they dance together. Their union together creates all that is in nature.

Your consciousness sees all of this as it unfolds. The witness in your subtle body is the Shiva, and the nature of the world around you is the Shakti. When the two are separate, you can't achieve spiritual awakening. When Shakti and Shiva merge, it will create the spiritual channel of oneness that the Kundalini will flow through. This is where you will achieve true happiness, and it can't be achieved while we are not united with the world we live in. This state of happiness is not conditional on your life, playing out in any particular pattern. The oneness and unconditional bliss that you will feel can only be achieved when you are at one with all people and all things in nature. You will not be separate from anything in creation.

Kundalini awakening is the concentrated energy of attention or awareness. It is the energy that manifests when your consciousness becomes free from all thought. You will experience more profound feelings of empathy with others. You will discover that you are more sensitive to the needs of others. You will know things profoundly, and you will probably develop psychic abilities. You will have more energy, and the aging process will most likely slow in your body and mind. You will have internal knowing and great peace as your charisma and creativity increase. As you become more of a part of all that is, you will see that all of the great mysteries of life aren't all that mysterious.

Realign your Prana (Life Force)

Your body is made up of pathways through which your energy flows and moves. The point that flows through these pathways is your prana, your life force. You will be able to harness this life force as you learn to awaken and control your Kundalini. This energy can be used to support you and heal you. It works on all levels, spiritually, physically, emotionally, and mentally. Power is a universal concept among all people. It is the undeniable force that allows for the existence of life and allows life to flourish. Western thinking people do not often embrace the concept of energy as it pertains to life and health. Many of the ancient health practices of Eastern medicine use power as a remedy for common physical and mental ailments. It can be used to supplement the most prescribed medications that are already known to work to restore health. This is known as energy healing, and it is the best way to realign your life force.

Depending on the method that you use, healing with energy focuses on the force of life that flows through everyone. This force dictates your ability to connect with other people as well as your strength, health, and mood. In some cultures, this energy is called qi or ki, pronounced as *chee*. Some cultures refer to it as prana. However, it is called; it is the supernatural force that cannot be seen or comprehended in the sense of worldly things. Western medicine and science are beginning to be more receptive to the idea of energy as a method of healing. They are beginning to embrace the principles behind the benefits and techniques that eastern cultures have been using for centuries. Your body runs on energy for every function it does, and your body is made of life. There is also a field of energy that surrounds every person. Being able to influence the flow of energy by using mental intention and awareness and physical abilities will bring you profound results. Your energy body can be altered through exercise, physical touch, and meditation to give you higher levels of energy, consciousness, and health. Techniques for healing your life will help you find the correct approach for you that will lead you on the right path to sustained health and healing.

Qigong – The concept of qi has led to a fundamental practice of energy exercise and healing that is known as qigong. This practice balances the flow of energy through the entire body by using meditation, breathing, and body postures to cultivate the force of life. Since it helps to develop muscle strength and agility, and balance, it is often used as a foundation practice for many of the martial arts disciplines. People who practice qigong want to develop a clearer vision of their purpose in life, as well as reducing their anxiety and finding greater awareness of the world around them and their place in it. The controlled movements are slow and are particularly useful in working with the elderly and those who engage in rigorous sports. The activities are meant to ease tension in the body and develop stability. Qigong opens up the meridians that have been blocked in the body by stress, poor health, injury, or anything else that the body deems as traumatic. These are the routes that the qi needs open so that it can flow freely through them. This openness will make room for the unimpeded movement of energy throughout your body. The philosophy behind qigong is that disease and illness are caused by your life being blocked. When you open up these passages, then you will be able to open the meridians to allow healing energy to flow through when you are sick, or even to prevent the disease from developing.

Reflexology – The focus of the ancients in the east to balance the flow of qi led to the development of reflexology. This practice targets the feet, ears, and hands primarily. It is believed that different systems in your body have a direct connection to other spots on your hands and feet. These can be detoxed and influenced positively to open up the meridians that make those direct connections. Reflexology opens up your energy blockages by encouraging the flow of lymph through relaxation of the muscles and stimulation of pressure points. This manipulation is done with an intense massage that is targeted at a specific area. This method of realigning your life force is thought to increase the circulation in your body as well as balance your energy, boost your immune system and cleanse your body of built-up toxins. The immediate physical effects of a session of reflexology might disappear quickly, but the internal results are unseen and will last a much longer time.

Chakra Healing – The Crown Chakra is the top of the seven internal chakras that the Kundalini must pass through on its way to the Crown Chakra. These are the centers of energy in your body. The seven chakras are thought to resemble seven wheels spinning with power since the word chakra means wheel. The location of the individual chakra in your body will determine what endocrine glands it connects to and which part of the nervous system it controls the function of. They are believed to function much like the meridians in the body for allowing energy to flow through. Your seven chakras are located along your spine from the base of your spine up to the top of your head. They function in a synchronized pattern to allow the energy of the Kundalini to flow through your body. The energy in your chakras must all be balanced because it would not work if one chakra were dull, and the next one was over-energized. The chakras can open and close, which helps to control the flow of energy. If you experience anger, sadness, and negativity, your chakras will likely close themselves. You will use intention, meditation, and breathing to be able to open up your chakras to allow the flow of positive energy and eliminate any negative energy that might be there.

Acupuncture – Ancient cultures teach that the meridians are a map of different routes in your body that allow energy to flow freely through your body. These meridians correspond with specific points where the nervous system, endocrine glands, and muscles interconnect with each other. The acupuncturist uses thin needles to pierce some of the more than six hundred points on the human body that will connect directly with body systems and major organs. These connections are made through the meridians and through the vessels that are associated with the meridians and are known as collaterals. In Chinese culture, the people who know these collaterals and meridians are highly revered. It is believed that acupuncture will help improve the function of your organs and relieve pain in your body by releasing particular adrenal hormones that deal with reducing pain and inflammation. Of all of the different forms of eastern medicine, acupuncture is the one that is most often used in conjunction with western medical practices. Even though needles are used in acupuncture it is often highly relaxing and is considered to be virtually painless.

Reiki – This is a more recent method of eastern healing based on five unbreakable principles: be kind to others, work hard, be grateful, do not worry, and do not become angry. The basis of reiki is the idea that the life force that flows through you can heal you and make you more conscious of your health. It is a method of self-discipline and self-improvement. The idea is to take an active role in healing yourself and keeping yourself healthy while you incorporate the healing qualities of energy into your life. Reiki is based on spirituality, but it is not a religious practice. It is based on the concept of the unseen force of life that flows between all people. That life force can be used for beneficial means when it is properly channeled. Practitioners of Reiki will use hand-on methods of healing to realign energy by balancing it in your body and transferring it to where it is needed the most.

Reject Negativity

Whether you chose to believe in them or even acknowledge them, there are negative entities in your world. The worst kinds of them will live in the lower frequencies of your spirituality. Negativity is attracted to specific types of emotional and mental energy, and it is drawn into different forms of thought that are determined by the content that comes from these emotions. Negative entities are usually not able to be seen by the human eye, but they are felt in your subtle body. They will affect your physical body in ways that can drag down your spirits and can make you physically ill. Those who have already experienced the awakening of their Kundalini will be better able to see these negative entities and to resist their powers. When you are awakened, you will be better able to see or perceive the negative entities lurking in your world because you will be better able to access a broader spectrum of hearing subtle frequencies.

Sometimes a negative entity will attach to a particular person because they are on the same frequency, and their thoughts and feelings are compatible. Some will enter your subtle body because of your attitude and the vibration that you are emitting at a particular moment. Others will come in because of the meditation or dream you had or a particular psychic state that you are in. You might pick up a negative entity while you are traveling a different astral plane or having an out-of-body experience. If you frequently indulge in highly negative forms of entertainment, then you will most likely draw in negative entities. You can become the target of negative entities and psychic predators when you have insufficient internal energy or low self-discipline or esteem.

When negative entities attach themselves to you in a dream, they will enter through a dream sequence or a symbolic vision. This dream may feature scenes or people that you do not recognize that are operating in a dream that looks entirely plausible as if it really could happen. An experienced or awakened person would notice the subtle differences in the vision that points to the fact that it is not reality. These encounters can bring in negative energy as a result of the life that is exchanged between the dreamer and the dream, and these can transfer negative entities over to the spiritual body of the dreamer. This will result in contamination of your mind, and your subtle body as your positive energy is pulled back into the origin of the negative entity, to fuel further dreams and future negative entities.

Sometimes you will create your negative entities. These will come from evil or unhealthy intentions, attitudes, behaviors, or actions. You might do nothing more than laugh at a situation that is not appropriate for laughter, and this would be enough to create a malicious entity. Your thoughts have the power and the ability to manifest themselves as thought forms, and these will be either positive thoughts or negative thoughts, depending on the particular idea that is involved. The intention of the view and the ultimate content will manifest the belief in the spiritual world.

Those negative energies that have already been created will wait around in places of low power for a person who is down on energy to come near. They will then attach themselves to that person. These negative entities will first enter the aura that surrounds the person, their auric field. If they find the opportunity, they will enter the subtle body through holes in the person's aura, primarily if the negative energy and the person are operating on the same frequency. Malicious entities can enter one person through close physical contact with another person. Most people are entirely unaware that this is happening until the happening is over, and the negative entity has attached to them and is affecting their thoughts and feelings.

By expelling the negative entities, you will be able to banish the negativity from your life, which is vital to do when you are attempting to awaken your Kundalini. When you realize a malicious entity has taken over, you can create positive thoughts to drive it away. Negative and positive can't live together in the same space, so the positivity will eventually overcome the negativity. Keeping the negative entities inside will only serve to contaminate your mind and your subtle body. But ridding yourself of negative entities is not always as simple, rejecting the negative things in your life.

Because you may believe that Buddha or Jesus never had any negative thoughts, you may think that you should not have any either. But this is not possible, because you are human and you have the ideas of a human. If you knock yourself down whenever you have a negative thought, then you will merely be judging yourself in ways you should not be judging yourself.

You have negative thoughts, and these negative thoughts carry negative energy. They do bring negative energy, but that energy will only go as far as you allow it to go. If you continuously strive not to have negative thoughts, you will only have more of them. It is like trying not to eat junk food – the more that you think about not eating junk food, the more you are thinking about junk food and wanting to eat it. So when you have a negative thought, feel its energy and then let it go. The secret is not to act on negative thinking because working on it will give it a life of its own. The goal of the inner growth needed to awaken your Kundalini is not to become an entirely positive person but to realize that you are free to think and feel on your own, no matter what the circumstances are around you. When you know that you are free to think as lively or as unfavorable as you want to feel, then the negative entities will no longer hold any power over you because they will no longer interest you. Then the real you can shine positively forward.

Access Your Central Channel

When your Kundalini first awakens, you will feel it somewhere in the region of your tailbone, and you might feel a tingling sensation as it begins to creep up your spine. Awakening Kundalini is quite different from just awakening your energy because the first few times the Kundalini travels up your spine, it may feel something like a small volcano has erupted inside of you. Kundalini will work its way up the center of your spine until it encounters some sort of blockage. It will typically find some type of significant blockage in one of the lower three chakras.

Your Kundalini is highly intelligent, and it will continue to work its way through cycles. It will travel back to the first chakra, the Root Chakra, and then back to its point of origin until it can pass through the Root Chakra unimpeded. It will continue to go through these cycles of dormancy and activity until it can rise through all of the lower six chakras. The effort you put into awakening your Kundalini will be reflected in the power of the Kundalini as it is awakening. If you put more effort into it, then it will be able to open the blocked chakras faster and more efficiently. However, you will feel the effects of this in the release of stored emotions that may cause spiritual, emotional, and physical pain.

When the Kundalini energy has reached the Crown Chakra and unblocked it, then it will have achieved its ultimate goal, and it will be fully awake. When the Kundalini first begins awakening, it is coiled into a tight knot at the base of your spine. When it is fully uncoiled, it will rise out of the Crown Chakra, and you might feel the explosion of energy in your head. You will experience a host of spiritual, mental, and physical changes that might make you feel as though someone or something close to you has died. If you think about it, there has been death for you. It is the death of the way you saw yourself before the awakening and all of the impressions you held about yourself.

The Kundalini will continue to arise through your central channel that is now open and receptive to healing energy. You may feel an intense rush or a gentle wave; the feeling will differ according to what is needed at that moment. Kundalini is a conscious form of energy that is unique to the current situation. You might need to experience another massive rush of energy that flows through your central channel and clears out large amounts of leftover material that is stuck there. You might need the Kundalini to hang out in your Root Chakra, building the vital force that is required to provide the foundation for your physical and subtle body. Whenever the Kundalini is needed longer in any one chakra, it will simmer there as long as it is required to.

Once Kundalini has completed its flow to the Crown Chakra, it will then flow into the primary channels of the body. It will then begin to flow to all of your cells, tissues, and organs. This flow will help to give every part of your body a sense that it is vibrating and glowing. Then the central column will develop if it hasn't already. You will feel that there is a column of energy that extends from the ground underneath your feet up into the air above the top of your head. At first, this will be nothing more than a small column, but it will eventually widen to encompass your entire aura, surrounding your body and your auric field.

When your central channel is open, and you can experience the chakras above and below you, then you will be more connected to your essential nature. You will then be able to realize all components of your humanity and enjoy every part of yourself. This empathy will include all of your thoughts and emotions. Sometimes people will stop before they reach this stage because they are afraid of the openness they feel when their Kundalini is completely awakened and energized. Awakening your upper and lower chakras will allow you to explore deeply your inner chakras, especially the lower ones, and find comfort in your emotional and primal drives.

Visualization

You can use visualization of the Kundalini awakening as a method for bringing life to your Kundalini and letting energy flow freely through your subtle body. The best way to do this is to guide yourself through a practice of meditation that will awaken your Kundalini.

You will begin by sitting comfortably somewhere that you can be quiet, and you will not be disturbed. If you are disturbed during your meditation, it will not work as well, or at all, and you will be left feeling frustrated. It can be difficult enough to practice meditation without any disturbances, so set the scene for you to be successful. Make sure that your environment is ideal for you to relax in. It should be quiet and peaceful, you should be comfortable, and you need to be able to relax your mind and body completely.

Straighten your spine so that you are upright but not rigid. Let your stomach relax and close your eyes entirely but not tightly. Set the focus of your attention on your breathing. Let your breathing naturally slow, which might take a few minutes to accomplish. You want to breathe in and out evenly and deeply as soon as your breathing is deep and regular, set the focus of your attention on your spine. Your spine should be straight. Let your focus travel down your spine until your thoughts rest on the area at the base of your spine. Visualize the bottom of your spine, and begin to see yourself breathing from the base of your spine. As you exhale and inhale, see in your mind that your breaths are coming from the area at the bottom of your spine. Continue your breathing in this manner for a few minutes to establish that your breath is coming from there.

Once you feel that your focus is concentrated enough, see in your mind's eye a small black cylinder with the top removed, and the cylinder is resting at the base of your spine. Visualize a little red baby snake coming out of this cylinder, waving its head from side to side as it explores its surroundings. The baby snake opens its mouth and looks upward toward the top of your spine, hissing while it is investigating. As the baby snake rises along with your spine, picture that its mouth is as large as your entire body, as though it could swallow you whole if it wanted to. As the body rises, the tail will remain near the bottom of the spine. Continue your meditation while you imagine this. During this time, the serpent will often rise and fall back, growing a bit farther with every effort. You will know that your meditation has been successful when you feel enormous feelings of peace and serenity, or when you feel an explosion of energy rising along your spine.

This meditation uses many of the critical aspects of methods for awakening the Kundalini. Doing the meditation will allow you to develop your power of visualization and your powers of concentration. As your awareness becomes more defined, you will become more aware of your chakras and their management. You will also develop the ability to control your breathing and to incorporate your breathing techniques into other areas of your body. You will be able to cleanse your chakras and your channels.

Sometimes when you practice meditation, you will not feel the effects immediately, and you will probably not be successful in the beginning. As you continue to meditate, your chakras and channels will become even more evident each time so that eventually all blockages have been pushed away, and your subtle body is free to be filled with healing energy.

Breathing and Good Posture

People who are just beginning on their practice of meditation often get sidetracked by the idea of breathing. It is normal to wonder if there is a right way to breathe while you are meditating. Most of the meditation experts will recommend that you just let your body breathe naturally. The best way for you to breathe while you are contemplating is for you to breathe the way you usually breathe. If you can push yourself to breathe a bit more deeply, to be able to fill your lungs with more air and your body with more energy, then do so, just don't worry if you can't do it in the beginning. Meditation is not a goal that you need to reach, it is a practice, and you should practice as often as possible.

Part of practicing meditation is to learn to practice mindfulness, and this includes being mindful of your breathing. In your daily life, it is too easy to get caught up in thinking of all of the tasks that are waiting for you to do. When you meditate, you should only be thinking of yourself and your meditation. Following this rule will empty your mind of the stress, anxiety, and distraction that everyday life brings to you.

When you practice mindful breathing during meditation, you will need to pay close attention to your exhalations and inhalations. As you breathe, you will feel different sensations flowing through your body, and you should let your mind enjoy these sensations. See how your chest and your tummy move as you breathe. If they should begin to wander away, bring your thoughts back to your breath. It is usual for your mind to stray, but when you get it back, you are practicing mindfulness. If you can do this for just fifteen minutes every day, you will begin to notice a radical change in how you feel. The simple act of meditation will significantly improve your quality of life. When your mind has learned contentment from meditation, you will have a more positive perception of the world. You will also make better decisions and find more in life to appreciate.

No matter what form your meditation takes, the benefits that you reap will be numerous and unquestionable. When your thoughts are calm, you will be more peaceful, and you will feel happier. It will take time for you to feel the more profound benefits of your meditation, but those benefits will come with time. When you are just beginning, you should only commit yourself to a short period of reflection, like five or ten minutes daily. This is a manageable amount of time for anyone to commit to, and it will get you into the regular daily practice of meditation.

When you have settled yourself into your meditation position, set your focus on your breath as you exhale and inhale. Don't spend any time trying to modify or time your breathing, but just let your breath go in and out in its natural rhythm. You will do your best when you relax and concentrate on one breath coming at a time. If thoughts distract you, acknowledge them and then return directly to your breathing. In the beginning, it can be conducive if you count breath cycles. Begin at the end of an exhalation and calculate the next inhalation and exhalation as one breath cycle. Count the cycles one by one until you reach ten cycles, and then begin again at one. Your goal is not to improve your counting or to try and see how high of a number you can reach. Your goal is to teach you and encourage you to be mindful of your breathing.

After you have spent some time counting your breaths, then enjoy the breathing itself. Watch your chest as it contracts and expands with the air going in and out. Feel your lungs expand and contract. If you practice your breathing techniques regularly and become more mindful of your breathing, then your meditation will deepen and improve with time.

Good posture is essential for good meditation. You do not need to sit on the floor and contort your body into impossible positions. Sit wherever you are most comfortable, and unless you are already a master at yoga positions that will probably be in a chair, or at least on a cushion if you choose to sit on the floor. If you decide to sit in a chair, try not to sit with your back relaxing against the end of the chair, because this position will encourage too much relaxation. It is best to sit more upright, setting a large pillow or a cushion behind your back if needed. Part of meditation is in the body, and if your body is not awake and alert, your meditation will be sluggish and unproductive. Following the basic guidelines for the position of your body that will help you be properly seated and aligned. You should either close your eyes or focus your gaze on a point about six feet in front of you. To keep your cervical spine in alignment, you should keep your chin tucked in slightly. Let your spine follow its natural path, and if it curves a bit, that is okay. Keep your bottom, your sitting bones, stable and centered under your body. Let your palms rest gently on your thighs as your arms are relaxed beside your body. If you cross your legs, keep them loose, with your knees below your hips.

To achieve the primary seated position for meditation, just follow these guidelines. Your body will tense up if your seat is not comfortable, and this will make your meditation difficult. Put your bottom directly in the center of the chair or cushion where you are sitting. Rock back and forth on your bottom when you first sit down, as this will loosen up your sitting bones and allow them to find stable ground for sitting. Once the sitting bones are comfortable, the remainder of your posture will fall into place easily. If your spine is slouched or arched during meditation, your body will fall out of alignment. This will cause your body to strain and feel stiff, and then your mind will find it difficult to concentrate. When you sit down, let your body drape forward at first, and then slowly straighten your spine after your sitting bones are settled. This lets all of your vertebrae in your spine stack on top of each other as you straighten up. You will feel strain in your neck, back, and hips if you sit with your knees above your thighs, so make sure you are sitting where your bottom is above the level of your knees. This might mean that your meditation will be done with you sitting in a chair, and there is nothing wrong with that.

Because your mind tends to be more alert when you are sitting up, it is recommended that you do not meditate while you are lying down. But this is simply a recommendation. If you have any reason that makes sitting uncomfortable, then feel free to do your meditation while you are lying down. Just try to lie flat on your back so that your breathing will be as open as possible.

The point of practicing meditation is to learn to bring the quality of mindfulness into your daily life. Most people spend too much time locked in an office, curved over in front of a computer or a desk. Meditation will allow you to realign your body and bring peace and relaxation into your life.

Once you have awakened your Kundalini, you will experience such a difference in your everyday life. You will find life is no longer mundane as you begin to enjoy the beauty of it every day. You will soon feel a level of energy like you have never known before. And you will feel so free!

CHAPTER 3

Accessing Kundalini Through Open Chakras

The seven internal chakras that lie along your spine are the confined pools of energy that govern your physical health and psychological qualities. The three lower chakras govern your instinctual thoughts and feelings, and the four upper chakras govern your mental and spiritual properties. You need all seven of the chakras to be functioning on the same level of energy so that they will contribute equally to your health and well-being. Your thoughts and feelings need to join forces with your instincts to create the whole you. You can't achieve true inner peace and feel real energy until all of your seven chakras are correctly balanced. The Kundalini will flow through the seven chakras to bring life to the entire body, so all seven chakras must be open to allow the energy of the Kundalini to flow through freely. Since each chakra is individual and separate from the other six, even though they depend on each other and they work together, each chakra will require unique activities to open it and keep it healthy.

The Root Chakra

The foundation of your seven internal chakras is your Root Chakra. It is the body's foundation for overall well-being and good health. You will feel stability, trust, relaxation, security, and prosperity when this chakra is open and healthy. You will think clearly in all areas of your life as well as enjoying plenty of energy. Feeling prepared for the complications of life, as well as feeling centered and calm, are all characteristics that mean that your Root Chakra is open and healthy. You will be mentally and physically at ease with yourself, as well as possessing a great deal of common sense.

When your Root Chakra is not healthy, you will suffer from physical disorders of your lower body. You might suffer from constipation and diarrhea. You can also suffer from anxiety, eating disorders, aches and pains in random places in your body, and chronic illnesses. You will be hampered by feelings of aggression, vulnerability, insecurity, paranoia, and a general inability to truly relax. You might feel that your life is a constant struggle to succeed and that you never really achieve any of the goals that you set for yourself. There are many different ways that you can heal the Root Chakra.

Since red is the corresponding color of the Root Chakra, you will want to focus on incorporating this color into your life as much as possible. When you are meditating, try to imagine a red pool of warm liquid spreading around the base of your spine and covering your Root Chakra in its warmth. Imagine this pool spreading to protect your Root Chakra and the area that surrounds it. Meditate with red cloths covering your area or red candles lit nearby. The Root Chakra also likes the scents with earthy essences like patchouli, sandalwood, and frankincense, so burn these scents as often as possible as incense or with using essential oils in an oil burner. Your Root Chakra also prefers foods that are in the red color family, and it also likes any root vegetable. Fill your diet with beets, onions, carrots, apples, and cherries. Use the gemstones that are red or black to decorate your home and garden, like red jasper, garnet, red carnelian, bloodstone, jet, smoky quartz, and hematite.

You will want to engage in any physical activity that uses the lower body to heal the Root Chakra, particularly standing yoga poses and any dancing. Go for a walk and feel all of the energy from nature seeping up into your legs. If you can walk on grass or sand in your bare feet, then that is even better.

Write down in a journal the things you are doing to heal your Root Chakra, especially the ones that are helping you. Keep note of the things that you need in your life so that you will feel well supported, and also note the items that are supporting you. Think about your roots and how strong they can be, especially ties to your family, friends, and the community. Write down your dreams and goals, and make note whenever you are successful.

When you have opened and healed your Root Chakra, you will then have a strong foundation for your health. This will also provide you with a strong foundation for your other chakras, and it will help you open and heal them. As your Root Chakra grows in strength you will feel more confident and energetic, and you will no longer be driven by guilt and fear. You will then be driven by the knowledge that your life will be just fine, and it will work out the way you want it to be.

The Sacral Chakra

This is the internal center of your creative, emotional, and sexual energy. The physical sensations in your body, as well as your feelings, thoughts, and actions, will let you know when your Sacral Chakra is healthy and when it needs healing. If it needs healing, then you will probably have illnesses or disorders of your lower back, kidneys, and your stomach. Your creativity will be stagnant, and you will overthink everything. You will feed on the drama that others bring to you, and you will either be overly sensitive or overly aloof. Exhaustion will regularly overwhelm you because you will have no energy, and you will likely suffer from sexual tensions and reproductive problems. You will be overly emotional or utterly lacking appropriate emotions. Feeling that you are deprived of any real pleasure in your life will cause you to seek pleasure anywhere that you can find it, which will likely mean that you will be addicted to work, gambling, compulsive shopping, drugs, food, drink, or sexual activity.

A healthy Sacral Chakra will leave you feeling pleased with yourself and comfortable in your skin. You will enjoy being a sexual creature in ways that are healthy for you and well-balanced. Life will not need to be excessive to bring pleasure to you. You will find it easy to be emotionally open with others while remaining emotionally grounded. You will find great joy in the small things in life once again, and your levels of creativity will soar. There are many good ways to heal your Sacral Chakra.

Look into trying new activities and ideas to spur your creativity. Try sewing, quilting, sculpting, drawing, painting, gardening, and photography, cooking, or making jewelry. The idea is to try anything that will light a spark of creativity in your mind and soul. If you find something that you enjoy doing, then take the time to pursue it, since many creative endeavors will take time to learn how to do them correctly. Review all of the ideas about sexuality that you knew when you were a child, and only keep the ones that suit your particular lifestyle. You do not need to live with the ideas and concepts that you learned when you were a child. Ideas about sexuality that do not make you happy will block your Sacral Chakra since it is the chakra that controls your sexuality and your sexual activity.

People will chase pleasure in meaningless or dangerous activities because they have holes in their lives, and they are seeking something to fill them. You might not even realize what it is that you are missing; you just know that something is not right in your life. This pursuit is how people fall into the habits that become addictions. This occasion is where you will need to spend some quality time getting to know yourself. Take the time to remember what was going on in your life when you fell into the addiction. Learn what your emotional triggers are.

Surround yourself with anything orange in color. Wear garments that are orange, or use orange rugs and throws as accent pieces around your house. Eat more of the foods that are orange in color like peaches, papaya, mangos, apricots, sweet potatoes, carrots, and oranges. Even the simple act of setting a bowl full of tangerines, nectarines, and oranges on your kitchen counter or dining room table will make you feel better.

You will also need to embrace the look that your body now has and stop hating it or putting it down. Change your physical appearance if you are not happy with it, but you need to be able to accept that you are working with the way you look right now. Use guided meditations, mostly to reaffirm your love for yourself. Drink some ginger tea or add more ginger to your foods. Do yoga poses that require bending and stretching or take an exercise class. Use essential oils in the fragrances that your Sacral Chakra will love, like orange, neroli, jasmine, ginger, bergamot, or rosewood. Get spontaneous and do things you would not normally do. Pay attention to what makes you feel good and then do more of those activities.

The Solar Plexus Chakra

This one is the third of the lower chakras. You will feel a tremendous inner drive and more self-control and self-confidence when your Solar Plexus Chakra is open and healthy. This chakra can become blocked by traumatic experiences that you have suffered, as well as from bad habits and stubborn mindsets. Some incidents might not seem traumatic to you, but your Solar Plexus Chakra feels that they were. If you were bullied as a child by other children, if your parents were strict authoritarian figures, or if you lived in any situation where the authorities were stringent, then your Solar Plexus Chakra is probably damaged. If you had ever suffered from mental, sexual, emotional, or physical abuse in your lifetime, mostly when you were a child, then your Solar Plexus Chakra is probably blocked or unhealthy.

Your Solar Plexus Chakra is the very center of your willpower and your self-esteem. It needs to be functioning well if you are to be performing well. All of the internal energy that is associated with your actions, intentions, identity, and vitality are directly regulated by your Solar Plexus Chakra. If you need to open or heal this chakra, then you will most likely carry a lot of excess weight around the middle of your body. You can also have diabetes, ulcers, irritable bowel syndrome, and hypoglycemia. You will almost always feel significant fatigue, and you will still be too hot or too cold. Since you will have difficulty forming personal boundaries, then most of your relationships will probably be built on codependency. You will either bully other people or try to dominate others because of your inflated ego, or you will always seek approval from other people because you will suffer from low or no self esteem. You might be addicted to one or more substances because you are either manipulative or weak and powerless.

You will live a harmonious life full of self-confidence when your Solar Plexus Chakra is open and healthy. You will trust in your abilities, and you will be quite comfortable in your skin. You will understand the power that you possess, and you will be satisfied with using it correctly. You will create healthy boundaries for yourself because you will feel more assured in your worth. You will no longer have episodes of explosive anger or times when you minimize yourself because you will respect yourself and other people. You will lose your lethargy and your tendencies toward addiction because you will once again have the energy to drive your performance. You will be energized, focused, empowered, and ready to achieve your goals and seek your dreams.

Essential oils can be used to help open and heal your Solar Plexus Chakra, especially cinnamon, black pepper, rosemary, clove, sandalwood, and cypress. Put several drops of one of these diluted essential oils on your wrists; wear a pendant diffuser as a lovely piece of jewelry, or put some oil into an oil burner and set it near you. You can carry individual crystals with you or wear them, like the tiger's eye, topaz, amber, citrine, and yellow calcite. Certain herbs like lemongrass, rosemary, or chamomile are excellent for opening and healing your Solar Plexus Chakra. You need to focus your diet on essential foods like lentils, spelt, oats, rye, beans, chickpeas, and rice, while using spices such as turmeric, ginger, cumin, and cinnamon.

You will also want to stay away from people who are overly judgmental or overly critical. If you are not able to completely cut ties with them, then limit your contact with them. Spend time with the kind of people who will help to support you and build you up. They will help you find your power and also help you to use it in the right way. Get out of your dull routine and try something new now and then, to add a little emotional spice to your life. You will find renewed levels of energy and get a boost of vitality if you even change one thing in your routine or change one or two of the people in your inner circle that are keeping you down.

You are no longer the victim that you once were. Now is the time to spend some quality time dedicated to learning who you are and what you want out of life. You are no longer powerless and defenseless. You will also no longer sacrifice your desires to make other people happy, just as you will no longer blame your actions on other people. You do not need to be rude just to refuse the ideas of others, but do it politely and go on. Pay attention to what makes you happy spiritually, mentally, and emotionally, and then do those things to take care of yourself, and your Solar plexus Chakra will take care of you.

The Heart Chakra

This is the chakra that is in the center of your physical body, it is the center chakra of the seven internal chakras, and it is also the spiritual and emotional center of your unity, balance, and love. You will feel open and connected to other people when your Heart Chakra is open and healthy. You will also feel receptive, accepting, forgiving, and generous. If your Heart Chakra is closed or unhealthy, then you will likely feel loneliness, resentment, bitterness, fear, and social isolation. Your Heart Chakra will suffer because of many different things. This chakra might need healing if you were raised by or are surrounded by people who are cold and unfeeling. If you have ever suffered from emotional or physical abuse, or if you were denied affection and love as a child, then your Heart Chakra will most likely need healing. And if you harbor unhealthy attitudes and beliefs about the way that love should be or if you have habits that are self-destructive, then your Heart Chakra is probably suffering.

Your Heart Chakra is responsible for regulating the energy in your subtle body that is associated with self-acceptance, compassion, self-love, openness, and the love that you feel for other people. It is the center of your love and emotional balance and the guide to your connections and interactions with other people. When this chakra is healthy, it is open to receiving and giving love, as well as being cleansed, clear, and supportive of your ideals. When the Heart Chakra is unhealthy or blocked, you might suffer from illnesses in your chest with your heart or lungs, or you might suffer from diseases that are connected to these two organs like asthma, high blood pressure, and poor circulation. You will be suspicious of other people, and you will not trust their motives when it comes to your well-being. You will struggle to feel and give real love, so your relationships will most likely be built on codependency. You will continuously replay in your mind any trauma you have suffered in your life, and this might make you needy, anxious, fearful, and self-critical. Bitter thoughts and feelings will sometimes overwhelm you, and you will find it difficult to let go of them. Your style of love will swing wildly between being emotionally distant in your relationships and being utterly terrified of being alone.

The Heart Chakra loves the color green, so try to surround yourself with this color, especially if it takes you out into nature. Fill your home with as many houseplants as you can, and grow a garden if you have space. Use herbs like astragalus, rose, hawthorn, holy basil, nettle, and angelica to make sachets for your room or to carry with you. Use the heart healing crystals of jade, rose quartz, ruby, green fluorite, emerald, and malachite as jewelry for your person or as decoration in your home. Rose, marjoram, lavender, neroli, and angelica essential oil can be worn on the skin or burned in a burner for scented oil to give off the scents. Try to add more green heart-healing foods into your diet. Your Heart Chakra will love zucchini, spinach, kale, cabbage, kiwis, avocados, peas, broccoli, green apples, pears, Swiss chard, grapes, celery, and lettuce. And the yoga poses that are meant for healing, like the camel pose, fish pose, cobra pose, or the forward bend, are especially helpful.

Meditation will help to heal your Heart Chakra, especially meditation that is based on loving affirmations for yourself. Set personal boundaries and personal limits, because you don't need to be agreeable to all people all of the time. Count your blessings, and never take love and life for granted. It will be difficult for you to show love to others if you do not love yourself or if your mind is overly critical. Think of what other people might be going through, so that you don't take their actions personally all of the time. Embrace your own emotions, because there is nothing wrong with occasionally feeling bored, sad, unhappy, angry, or jealous, as long as you do not allow yourself to dwell on those feelings for too long. Allow yourself to give love to other people and receive love from them, and learn to accept compliments graciously.

The Throat Chakra

You will be able to be creative, honest, confidant, assertive, and not afraid to speak your truth when your Throat Chakra is balanced. When it is blocked or unhealthy, then you will have problems with dishonesty, stubbornness, social anxiety, and shyness, lack of trust in others, verbal aggressiveness, and a deep fear of expressing your inner feelings and thoughts out loud. When children are forbidden to express themselves in any usual way like verbally or creatively, if they are continuously criticized by the figures of authority in their lives, or if they are constantly belittled and made to feel worthless, then they will probably grow into people who have a blocked or unhealthy Throat Chakra. This chakra holds the energy that regulates your authenticity, creativity, and understanding.

When your Throat Chakra is blocked or unhealthy, then you might experience sinus infections, respiratory infections, or infections of the throat. You might suffer from hyperthyroidism or hypothyroidism, or your lymph nodes might be swollen continuously. Your voice might often break or sound nasally or thin, and you might have premature hearing loss or ear infections. You find honesty something that is too hard for you to subscribe to regularly, often doing one thing and saying something else. Your partner makes most or all of the decisions in your relationships since you are quiet and trying to keep the peace. You are either painfully shy or overly opinionated. Being misunderstood and suffering from miscommunications is no stranger to you.

You will want to begin to heal your Throat Chakra with meditations that focus on thoughts of love and acceptance of yourself as well as words that allow you to think or feel. Write your deepest, most private thoughts in a journal so that you will be in the regular habit of expressing your inner feelings. Surround yourself with things that are colored blue since this is the color of the Throat Chakra. Add more blue foods into your diet like grapes, currants, blueberries, blackberries, and plums. The Throat Chakra also likes peaches, lemons, grapefruit, apples, kiwis, lemons, pears, figs, and apricots. Use herbs to heal the Throat Chakra, like elderberry, spearmint, cinnamon, echinacea, fennel, and cloves, making any of these into a soothing tea, either by themselves or in combinations. Blue crystals that you can wear or carry include tanzanite, larimar, blue kyanite, azurite, aquamarine, and lapis lazuli. Always drink pure water and use the essential oils eucalyptus, frankincense, neroli, clove, rosemary, and myrrh.

Release the energy that might be built up in your physical throat by laughing, screaming, or singing. Tune-up the voice of your subtle body by sitting in silence, especially under a clear blue sky or near a body of water. Try to practice being more assertive when you are alone. Try to speak kindly, but forcefully, when dealing with other people.

The Third Eye Chakra

All of the energy that is associated with your perceptions, thoughts, realities, and intuitions are centered in your Third Eye Chakra. A doorway to divine spiritual enlightenment is opened when your Third Eye Chakra is open and healthy. You will possess strong intuition, clarity, insight, self-awareness, and emotional balance when your Third Eye Chakra is open and healthy. If this chakra is closed or unhealthy, then you will most likely suffer from paranoia, anxiety, cynicism, mental illnesses, depression, and mood swings, and disorders. If you were a child who was taught never to question authority, or anything else, then your Third Eye chakra is probably blocked or unhealthy.

Physically this chakra controls your face and its parts, so when it is blocked or unhealthy, then you will probably suffer from earaches, problems with your vision, migraines, and sinus issues. Your temperament will either be arrogant and opinionated or dreamy and ungrounded. You will find it difficult to be open-minded because your stubbornness will regularly get in your way. Since you usually mistrust other people or automatically dislike them, the bulk of your relationships and interactions with other people will be trivial and superficial. You will have rigid ideas about how the world should be run and how people should behave. You will find it difficult to connect to your deeper self or your soul because you will not view reality as clearly as you need to to be open with yourself. You might also find yourself to be addicted to anything that will bring you feelings of pleasure.

If you genuinely want to open this chakra and make it healthy, then you will need to be willing to seek out and explore new and different points of view. This will help you break the pattern of being rigid and close-minded in your thoughts and beliefs. You will also need to practice grounding yourself, in reality, to avoid being lost in fantasy and delusion. Don't let your mind wander too often, as you need to practice mindfulness and keep yourself grounded in the present. Healing the Third Eye Chakra will require quite a lot of soul-searching and soul growth, and this will help you to feel more compassion for other people. You will also find it easier to reach your mystical state of being.

Spending time in bright sunlight will help you clear your mind and heal your Third Eye Chakra. When you are cooking, try to use herbs like saffron, basil, star anise, mugwort, jasmine, lavender, rosemary, lotus, or passionflower, or use them to burn as incense. You can also make delicious teas out of any of these herbs. Purple is the color of the Third Eye Chakra, so try adding more purple foods to your diets like blackberries, prunes, dates, raisins, figs, purple cabbage, blueberries, purple kale, and purple carrots. The essential oils that are appropriate for healing this chakra are frankincense, patchouli, sandalwood, juniper, vetiver, and clary sage. And you will want to carry or wear crystals of sapphire, shungite, lapis lazuli, amethyst, and kyanite. Standing forward bend and child's pose are the right yoga positions for healing this chakra.

The Third Eye Chakra will be damaged if you continuously hold onto core beliefs that limit your thinking. These are the deep convictions that you have about your fears, insecurities, and self-esteem. You will never be able to fully open and heal the Third Eye Chakra if you can't uncover the self-limiting beliefs that you are holding on to. You must be more self-aware if you want to heal this chakra. When you continue to identify with specific thoughts or feelings just because you have always held them, without really understanding why then you will find it impossible to heal this chakra. You need an open and healthy Third Eye Chakra to help you interpret your dreams and to reach out to other realms of possibility. And always tell yourself how well you are doing, especially when you can use phrases that describe how you see or create.

The Crown Chakra

This chakra is the uppermost of the seven internal chakras and the ultimate goal of the Kundalini. On a cosmic level, it is the energy center of your conscious thought. This chakra will connect you to the divine because it is the location of your real awareness. You will connect more quickly to your higher self when the Crown Chakra is open and healthy. You will tap into your inner wisdom, feel connected to other people and all of nature, see the larger picture more efficiently and feel an overwhelming sense of serenity and wholeness. If the environment that you are living in is full of trauma and stress, your Crown Chakra will most likely be blocked or unhealthy.

When this happens, you will probably suffer from neurological disorders or chronic illnesses of the endocrine system. You might be ultra-sensitive to bright light or suffer from migraines. You can experience delusions, insomnia, nightmares, night terrors, fog and mental confusion, and chronic fatigue. You will be a person who is very rigid in their thoughts and is materialistic, greedy, lonely, and spiritually disconnected. You will prefer to be isolated from other people, and your ego will likely be out of control because you don't feel any real care or compassion for other people.

Your access to enlightenment and the window to your soul is your Crown Chakra. When this chakra is open and healthy, then you will feel more inner peace and clarity as well as feeling more enlightened in your thoughts and feelings. You will feel a fantastic feeling of connection to all of humanity that will replace your former sense of isolation. You will finally belong to the universe. Life will once again be a beautiful thing since you will no longer be bored with it. You will live in the moment, and your reality will be defined by expansiveness and spontaneity.

Meditation is one of the fastest and easiest ways that you can heal your Crown Chakra. Spend some time allowing your thoughts to flow freely without trying to guide them. Watch movies and read books that you might not usually enjoy to broaden your horizons. Examine your feelings for those that deal with ignorance or prejudice, and get rid of them. You will spend less time on the thoughts and feelings that limit you when you enjoy more time with other people and trying to learn about other people.

You need to simplify your life by decluttering your immediate surroundings. An excess of belongings creates mess and clutter that will eventually lead to mental and emotional distress. You will be purifying yourself when you cleanse and simplify your environment. It is also essential while you are washing the physical space that you set aside a space for your daily meditations. These are vital for the health of your Crown Chakra. Put meaningful things in your meditation space, things like crystals, books, candles, or incense. Your spiritual practice might be unique to you, so you might want to write or read, pray or meditate, or sing or practice yoga or meditation.

You will want to spend time every day looking for signs from the divine signs that you are being communicated with by a higher power. Be open to the guidance that is coming from this source. This will help to open and heal your Crown Chakra so the Kundalini will have a receptive chakra to go to when it awakens inside you.

Kundalini and the Chakras

When the Kundalini awakens, it creates a free flow of energy that travels up through the chakras to the Crown Chakra, the top chakra of the seven internal chakras. When this energy leaves its dormant state at the base of your spine and travels upward, it creates an awakening that will lead to an expanded state of consciousness. When you open the central channel and open and heal the chakras to give the Kundalini free space to travel, the resulting experience will fill you full of life and energy far beyond any you have ever known.

CHAPTER 4

Signs Your Kundalini Is Awakened

A Kundalini awakening is a specific set of energetic experiences that will resolve all of the issues in your psyche. This experience will lead you to true enlightenment. Awakening your Kundalini will awaken the cosmic energy that is lying dormant inside of you. Once it is revived, it will create a gateway through your Crown Chakra, and it will connect you to an unlimited source of energy radiating from the universe. You can then tap into those energies so that you will be able to live a more full and fantastic life.

Many of the symptoms of a Kundalini awakening will come from changes to your nervous system. This makes it easy to confuse the symptoms of the awakening for some sort of neurological or biological condition you might be having. The symptoms of Kundalini awakening are signs that your body is trying to regain its balance or is trying to increase its levels of energy.

The symptoms of Kundalini awakening will happen all during the process. There will be symptoms during pre-awakening, at the actual spiritual awakening, and after the Kundalini awakening. All of these symptoms will lead you to a complete Kundalini transformation. After each event of a change, your body will produce signs of the physical changes. The interval between the episodes will not matter. Self-realization is not only a biological and spiritual process; it is also a gradual process. Since it is a gradual process, your ability to sustain your quiet mind during these processes will grow over time. Having a quiet and peaceful mind is crucial to gaining a full Kundalini awakening. The longer the period that you can maintain a calm mind, the stronger the symptoms of your Kundalini transformation will be. If you are progressing continuously in your spiritual transformation, then your signs of Kundalini awakening will get closer together each time that you experience them. After the first big rush of awakening, your symptoms will continue non-stop until your transformation is complete, growing gradually stronger every day.

When you are in the pre-awakening stage, you will experience specific types of symptoms. These symptoms are often due to changes that are happening in your mind. You will have insights, vivid dreams, and visions. You can experience many changes in your beliefs of the Universe and your feelings about other people. The world will begin to look like a very different place for you. You might start to question the beliefs in religion that you have held since you were a baby. The growing energy is working inside of your mind to clear out certain aspects of how you see the world and how you see your place in the world. As your mind becomes quieter, your eyes become more open, and you begin to see everything more consciously.

You will feel a sudden rise in energy as your Kundalini begins to open. You will start to see nature differently, with vivid colors instead of flat shades of grey. Your overall perception will change. Time will seem to stand still, and you will be able to see the way everything in the Universe is interconnected easily. You will feel Kundalini awakening symptoms like flashes of light, rushes of energy, and overall warmth. You will now have vivid dreams and visions about things you didn't know before. It will seem as though the information is being downloaded to you from some unknown source. You will begin to receive information about your purpose in life and the lessons you will need for this lifetime. As the energy in your soul begins to blossom, you might be able to recall some of your past lives. There are as many different versions about the symptoms of a Kundalini awakening as there are people who have experienced an awakening because everyone will experience something unique. Your personal feelings and beliefs will profoundly influence your personal experience. One common theme is that everyone is suddenly able to see past their limitations and begin to enjoy the wisdom that comes from a higher power. There is an expanded sense of perception and sensory abilities. These heightened abilities will seem to fade over time, but that just means you have become used to the sensations and are more comfortable with them.

The symptoms you experience toward the end of your Kundalini awakening are mostly combinations of different healing reactions that your body is having. You may experience emotional problems or physical illnesses. It is not uncommon for people to feel unwell in the first days of the Kundalini awakening, but this is nothing more than your body getting rid of the negative energy as the positive energy of the Kundalini moves in.

Just before your Kundalini begins to open, you might feel specific symptoms that will let you know that the transformation is about to happen. These might be as simple as twitching muscles or tingling in the nerves. It might be as unusual as sporadic jerking of your limbs, cramps, pain in various areas of your body, or flashes of light before your eyes. When you feel these things, try not to panic, but take them for the positive signs that they are. When these begin, you will likely be able to hold your meditations for more extended periods and make them deeper. You will feel yourself falling into a state of trance during your meditations that is deeper than you have ever experienced before. You will probably try to fight the feeling because you will feel like you are losing control of your body. In essence, you will be losing control, but it will be to your higher self and not some unknown being that you would need to fear. Let yourself fall into this trance and feel your meditations deepen and strengthen. If you do not think your reflections are trying to deepen like this, it might merely mean that you are still stuck at an early stage of awakening. Everyone will awaken at their rate. You might want to try to convince yourself that you are farther along than you are, but remember to take your time with your awakening.

Because there is so much false information surrounding the Kundalini awakening, you might see that some of the symptoms are described quite colorfully and exaggerated beyond what they are. The majority of your symptoms will be due to changes happening in your central nervous system. When your Kundalini transformation is entirely happening, the symptoms will occur daily, and they will get stronger as you come closer to your full awakening. You will eventually come near the end of your awakening and reach a plateau, and then all of the symptoms you have been feeling will begin to settle down. The only things that won't subside are your awareness level and your vibration, and these will become stronger every day.

Emotional Turmoil

During and after your Kundalini awakening, you will need to be more mindful of your inner feelings and emotions. This might be the most difficult one to put into action. Awakening your Kundalini will require you to recognize and process the negative emotions you have, as well as be able to release them out of your body. Most people have never been taught how to do this. Negative emotions most often remain trapped in your mind, heart, and soul because you have been told it is not safe to deal with those feelings, so they must be kept locked away and never acknowledged. You have activated an unconscious defensive mechanism for keeping those feelings buried. As a child, people may have often told you to 'grow up,' 'stop crying,' or 'suck it up' so many times that you learned not to show those feelings to anyone. Unfortunately, this means not offering them to yourself either.

You internalized all of your negative feelings because you felt that something must be wrong with you for feeling them in the first place. But the only way to truly heal is to learn to feel the full extent of your emotions, and even though this can be challenging, you can teach yourself to unlock all of those buried emotions. Burying your pain and your negative feelings will only result in the development of emotional problems, chronic illnesses and diseases, depression, and various addictions. Your body and your mind are looking for ways to soothe the pain. While none of this is your fault, you will need to be willing to deal with all of it if you are ever going to heal.

Awakening your Kundalini will assist you on this journey since she will be the one to teach you how to dig out your buried emotions and bypass all of your defenses to begin the healing process. This will happen automatically as a by-product of your Kundalini awakening. This will all, unfortunately, begin without your knowledge, and when you realize it is happening, you will need to deal with it and not repress any of your feelings. This is where you will need to consciously accept that change will happen to you, and it will be for the better of you.

You will need to work on reprogramming your reaction to pain and your perception of pain in your body. Your mind has already been programmed to see problems as a type of distress that needs to be avoided. Your conscious mind would prefer to seek out pleasure and relief. This action helps you to be able to recognize when someone has crossed one of your boundaries. Now is the time when you will be forced to deal with the old pains that your Kundalini awakening will bring out. You will need to deal with these old emotions and not try to repress them again, because trying to push them back will only make the energy of the Kundalini fish them out again, and you will be caught up in a vicious cycle of fighting with yourself. Your defenses will naturally be alarmed and on high alert, but if you fight this process, you will be fighting an exhausting battle that you will eventually lose. If you continue to feel that pain is unsafe, and it is wrong for you to feel it, then you will be struggling to win a battle against yourself that will have no positive outcome. You will need to teach your mind that emotional pain means that this part of your life is beginning to heal. You will also need to realize that this is one of the most significant changes you will make on your spiritual journey. Since Kundalini awakening will activate your fight-or-flight response, this is an essential concept for your mind to accept.

You can begin to retrain your brain by making a list of all of the occasions where allowing pain to be what it has resulted in a bit of learning for you. Your mind will probably need some amount of convincing, and this is fine. You will need to try to believe in this idea and not just force your mind to accept it as a fact. You have most likely lived your entire life doing your best to fit in with the expectations you were given, but you will abandon yourself and your potential if you do not accept your emotions and feelings. Kundalini awakening will require you to be yourself and to be honest with yourself so that you can take all of the wounded parts of yourself and love them until they can heal.

So when your Kundalini is awakening, and you have strong negative feelings and emotions rising, you will need to deal with them. You can work on different things to acknowledge your feelings and begin to heal your emotions. You will find that not every emotion or feeling will require a lot of attention, so you will need to work on knowing which ones need you and which ones don't. Some of your emotions will be too intense to address directly. Be patient with yourself because dealing with your feelings instead of burying them is a new skill. You will need to work to practice this to be good. You can do specific things that can emotionally support yourself during your Kundalini awakening.

Start by asking yourself what you are feeling at this particular moment. Try to keep your answer to the question in one word, since this will be easier for you to deal with. Describe your emotion with words like angry, desperate, sad, frustrated, lonely, and so on. You might be feeling several different emotions all at the same time, and this is perfectly normal. Imagine that the Kundalini is a fire, crawling through the underbrush of your feelings. When real fire attacks a forest, all of the little woodland creatures will run away in fear and hide somewhere until the fire is over. The fire will burn off all of the dead brush that is decaying the forest. A Kundalini awakening is much like a fire coursing through your body, getting rid of all the deadly emotions that are rotting your soul. Once you have named all of your thoughts, you can begin to offer help and compassion to your inner child, who is struggling with all of these changes.

Feel the emotion or feeling without actively trying to get rid of it or resolve it. Ask your body where it is most feeling this emotion and then try to relieve the tension that is likely building in that body part. Your intention should be to meet this emotion with compassion, curiosity, and love. Let the feeling know that you don't mean to harm it or try to resolve it, that you want to let it be what it is. If you sit with an emotion or a feeling long enough, it should shift by itself and might even disappear. Either way, it will most likely lose most of its strength or its power to cause you pain. If the emotion doesn't go away on its own, then concentrate on it for a while. Feel it filling your body and breathe deeply and evenly so that your body will continue to be nourished while the emotion tries to take over. Give the feeling a name. Keep feeling it until it loses its power over you.

Try to express the emotion or feeling out loud. Sometimes emotions just want an outlet and a way to know they are being acknowledged. Write about the feeling in a journal or draw a picture of it. Ask the emotion of how it would like to be portrayed. Hold on to the feeling as long as you possibly can without trying to get rid of it. Some emotions will be stronger than what you can deal with in one experience. Anger is one of the most intense emotions and it usually will need more than one incident to rid you of it.

During and after your Kundalini awakening, you will be releasing deep emotions and a strong feeling that you may have kept repressed for many years. This might be very painful for you to do, but it is needed if you are to move along through your transformation to your true enlightenment. This new awakening will require you to leave old emotions and pains behind so that you can continue to grow and develop your unity with the Universe.

Repressed Memories

When a person is experiencing a traumatic event, their conscious mind will often shut itself off so that they are not forced to share the event as it is happening. It is a defense mechanism of the mind to protect the person from the traumatic event. But even though the person has no recollection of the event, their reason is still storing memories of the event in their subconscious. These are known as repressed memories, and they can directly affect you, even if you do not realize that they are causing an effect on your life. Some situations are more common for causing repressed memories like domestic abuse, physical violence, sexual abuse, wartime events, and traumatic injuries you suffer as the result of an accident. No matter what kind of event caused the block in your mind, the suppression of the event is essential to your mind because it will allow you to continue to function as though the event never happened.

Even though you might not remember a repressed event, it is still with you, and it will still affect your daily behavior. These memories will eat at your mind, staying far enough in the background that you are not consciously aware of them. But because those memories have no emotions associated with them since they are repressed, they can't be released from your mind, and you can't be healed of them. They exist, but to you, they don't live. The influence happens on the unconscious level of your mind, but the effect occurs at the conscious level of your mind. Those who were endured sexual abuse as children may overeat as adults because something in their mind is telling them that if they are unattractive, they will be safe from harm. You can't heal the effects of traumatic events until you can acknowledge them and deal with them.

When you experience a Kundalini awakening, everything about your mind and your soul will be open and alive. It will be impossible for you to fully feel the transformation if your mind is not fully open, and when your awakening is complete, your mind will be fully accessible. Your repressed memories will be triggered, and they will once again be opened for your scrutiny. They might not come all at once, because your awakening might not be completed all at once, but they will make themselves known to you. Certain sights, sounds, or odors might invoke an unpleasant reaction. You may have visions in your dreams. Your repressed memories are most likely to be revealed to you in your dreams because your brain likes to work on healing pathways and memories while you are asleep. When you have a vivid imagination, especially about repressed memory, it is just your higher-self beginning to send messages to your lower-self during your Kundalini awakening. There is a story that needs to be told and brought into your conscious thoughts.

You might be tempted to stop your Kundalini awakening at this point simply because unlocking the repressed memories is too painful, and you do not feel strong enough to go on. But don't stop here, because once you get past these memories unlocking, then you will be able to deal with them and get rid of them for good. You will need to trust that you have the power to complete this unlocking process. You have made so much progress at this point. Tell yourself that you are willing to do these things so that you can improve your life. You know that these repressed memories have been holding you back and causing you pain. Your repressed memories limit your abilities to live a full and happy life, and it is time to let them go forever. You don't need your mind to protect you from these memories any longer. Your awakening Kundalini will provide you with the energy that you need to work through this. You will feel pain, both emotionally and physically, while you are working through the repressed emotions and memories. Your Kundalini is opening the door and removing the blocks your conscious mind has erected. Now that you can see what is wrong, you have the power to correct it.

Physical Symptoms

Kundalini awakening has much to do with the changes that your mind and your emotions go through. But your body will also experience physical changes as part of the transformation that may be confusing to you. As long as you do not have any underlying medical conditions, all of these symptoms will be perfectly normal. The energies associated with spiritual awakening can cause some bizarre symptoms.

You might feel activity at the top of your head or pressure in different parts of your head. It can be quite common for you to feel a tingling, an itching, or a buzzing sensation around or in parts of your scalp and skull. The energy of the Kundalini awakening will cause subtle changes in the receptors that you use for downloading and learning information. You might feel a spirit guide communicating with you, but it will be in a different part of your brain than where you usually think sensations of your thoughts.

All levels of your focus may feel extra sensitive. You might begin to hear things at lower or higher frequencies than you did before the awakening. The colors that you see might be more luminous and more vivid than you remember. When you touch things, the feeling will be more intense than before, and the scents you smell may seem to be overpowering. You also might suddenly be able to taste different layers in your food, and tastes you are not used to tasting.

Your body might suddenly begin to have growing pains, those strange pains you might recall from your childhood. You might also feel strange aches, almost like you have the flu, or you might suddenly have a burst of unexplained energy. You might become bloated or have other digestive issues. You might see a change in your intimate desires. All of these symptoms are common reactions to the surge of energy you will feel during a Kundalini awakening.

Your weight might begin to change while you are going through your transformation. If you find yourself needing less food and sleep, then you might lose some weight, or you might gain a little if you find yourself eating and sleeping more. Your body will decide what it needs, and it will expect you to provide for its needs. And you may have strange cravings for different foods. Your body might be trying to tell you that it lacks a particular nutrient. Having a Kundalini awakening is not an excuse to eat everything in sight, but give in to a few of your cravings to soothe your body now and then.

Since you are experiencing a rebalancing on many different levels, you might feel physically dizzy sometimes. Your inner ear is a susceptible organ, and it controls your sense of balance. Feelings of dizziness might also be due to fluctuations in your blood pressure. Your body is also realigning itself, even down to your DNA on the cellular level, so your sense of balance might be a bit off. Be more deliberate in your actions, and try to pay attention to what you are doing in the present moment to help reduce the possibility of sudden falls.

You may be prone to episodes of intense rushes of energy. Your body will be resonating with the new powers of a higher frequency, which is one of the best and most exhilarating of all of the physical symptoms of a Kundalini awakening. The Kundalini needs to rise through the central channel that runs along your spine, which is where your internal chakras are located. As the energy from the Kundalini awakening travels up the central track, it will need to go through these chakras, and if they are blocked, the power will open them wide so that it can proceed. The chakra will be cleared, old memories in your cells will be cleared out, and your body will respond with joyous lightening in the form of a giant rush of energy. Unfortunately, since you are on a spiritual roller coaster ride, your periods of tremendous highs might be followed with periods of devastating lows that leave you feeling exhausted. Rest when you need to and remember that this will eventually pass.

You are now probably nourishing your body in better ways than you used to, and you get further into your transformation. You will be consuming more nutrients, and this will create positive changes in your body. One of the most effortless changes to see is that your hair and nails will probably begin to grow much more quickly than they used to. But along with this positive trend, you may notice some adverse food-related effects of the awakening, usually in the form of food intolerances and allergies you never had before. This might just be your body telling you that a particular food is no longer suitable for you because it does not nourish your new body in the way your body needs.

Humans are not usually fond of change, and they often feel moments of anxiety when things change that are beyond their control. Your Kundalini awakening will not be in your possession. A spiritual awakening will require you and your body to adjust on many different levels. Breathe evenly, deeply, and slowly, and try your best to keep your thoughts in the present when they begin to race and flutter all over the place. Take in the breath and focus on it; be thankful for the oxygen that is flowing into your lungs and filling your body. Remind yourself that these symptoms will pass and that you are entirely safe. You might also feel a bit of fogginess in your left brain. Your right mind is in charge of your creativity and your imagination. All of your intuitive thinking comes from the right side of your brain, that thinking that goes beyond logical thought and any impressions that your five senses might bring to you. The left brain is the analytical side of your mind. It is responsible for rational and linear thinking. Your right brain will surge forward quickly to align itself with the Kundalini awakening. Your left brain will most likely skip and stick because it doesn't quite know what to do in these situations. The feelings and emotions of the Kundalini awakening make no sense to your left brain, so that it might feel a bit foggy at times.

The energy of the Kundalini awakening might alter your sleeping habits. There will likely be nights when you are so full of life that you are unable to fall asleep or stay asleep. Then you will have nights when eight hours is nowhere near the amount of sleep that you need. During this time, you should rest when your body needs to, and try not to be too exhilarated when your body is experiencing a rush of energy. And don't feel bad if you need more sleep than usual. When you are sleeping is the time when your body heals itself from all of the things it has suffered during the day. It will also be more comfortable for your body to dump out the toxins that the Kundalini awakening is releasing if your body is well-rested.

As you move through the awakening experience, you might find periods when the look of your skin changes, especially the skin on your face. The energy that comes with the Kundalini awakening will improve your skin and make you look younger. The stress that you might sometimes feel during this period might make you look older than you are. And with all of the toxins of repressed memories and old intentions being released from your cells, your skin might undergo other changes, like the development of acne or eczema. These symptoms will pass as you work further through your transformation, and your skin will settle down once the toxins are cleansed away, and the energy levels balance out.

Self-Realization

At some point in your Kundalini awakening, you will come to realize that the Divine inspires your life. Your genuine reason for being is the relationship between the human part of you and the Divine part of you. When the boundaries of whatever spirituality or religion that you subscribe to are not enough to hold you any longer, when you begin to feel a hunger for your own spiritual experiences that are personally connected to you, then you have come to your self-realization.

The spiritual awakening you are experiencing is the beginning of your ascent toward really knowing yourself. This will help to emancipate you from the past illusions that have kept your psyche imprisoned in service to your false self. A Kundalini awakening is an emotionally spiritual experience that will take you to spiritual levels you only dreamed of before. You will find yourself trying to get rid of the principles that previously regimented you into submission. You will be like a new baby during your spiritual awakening, and you may feel quite vulnerable. You will not realize your enlightenment by trying to become anything in particular or pursue anything in particular. When you develop the ability to let go and be, it will come to you. You will need to let go of your ego and let your subtle body take control of you.

You will know you are achieving self-realization when you can let go of the fear the holds you tied to familiar things only because they are familiar. You probably have thoughts and emotions that do not serve any purpose to you, but you have hung onto them for so long that they have become a habit that you have kept. You have been kept in mental and emotional darkness by religious ideas and societal mores that were forced upon you. You fear being persecuted if you do not follow them, and you fear the unknown that is beyond the beliefs you subscribe to. But your desire to know true enlightenment is more potent than any fear you may be holding onto, so you take the risk and seek enlightenment and transformation. You found your inner courage and jumped feet first into the possibility that life will be better on the other side.

This journey has left you without any real sense of yourself, without the familiar beliefs and ideas that kept you grounded in your past reality. When you began to let go of your ego, you discovered that all of your boundaries and limits came into question. You are probably now wondering precisely who you are. And your transformation will provide you with many possible answers to that question. Every solution that you receive will send you seeking in a particular direction that may or may not be the way you need to go. And during your travels, your psyche will be struggling to pull you back together so you can be the person you were before the awakening began. If you have not yet started to venture out mentally and spiritually, know that it is coming. It happens to everyone who undergoes a Kundalini awakening. Your psyche chooses to continue to believe what it now believes. It is a rite of passage for you to seek your better self, and it requires new areas where you will need to grow and learn.

You will also find that a wide array of choices is now available to you. This Kundalini awakening will give you new insights into your life and the person you will become. You might feel the need to break new ground in an unfamiliar area. You might decide to become a teacher of the new way of life you will soon be enjoying, and you will spend time studying and learning. You might feel you must fight the old ideas with all the force of a rebel in a new land. You might even find that an alternative identity suits you better than the one you carry now. You can choose to be a shaman, seer, psychic, clairvoyant, or a medium; there will be many spiritual paths open to you and your talents. Be careful of what you decide to chase or take on during this time. Exploring new worlds is a marvelous thing to do, but if you take on a unique personality, it will be just another ego that you will need to get rid of. You will not truly enjoy your spiritual awakening until you can abandon all of your efforts to have a self. You won't need to replace your old self with any sort of new self, no matter how much better you think the new one might be. The truth is that the real you have always been you, and that is enough for the Universe. The Divine powers ask that you simply be you, without trying to wear any sort of mental or spiritual disguise.

Your spiritual awakening is your ability to transition to your next level of awareness, your self-realization. True self-realization will only happen when you can transition past the mistaken idea that you need to have some sort of definition that you need to be defined by a particular persona. You already have an identity, and that is you. You will not know or find your true self in the limits of your thinking mind. If you pursue your true self with the idea that you will merge yourself with it, then you will only succeed in creating another illusion. You are not able to integrate with what you already are. Trying to label yourself or define yourself will stand in the way of your true enlightenment. You are not only your physical body, but you are also not only your emotions, and you are not only your thoughts. You need to learn to let go.

When you have learned to let go of your ego, then your true self will be able to reveal your true nature through your open mind. When you know to stop trying to become someone, when you stop trying to identify with particular things when you stop trying to be someone, then your ego will melt away. These ego structures distort your sense of reality, and they need to be stilled so that your true self can shine through.

Empathic Abilities

Being an empath and this powerful spiritual awakening that you are undergoing are genuinely connected. You might have trouble imagining a time when your thoughts and emotions will be collected, calm, and balanced. You might feel as though you will never again enjoy a level of mental state or feel as though your sanity has returned. Although it may seem to be in the distant future, or maybe it seems impossible right now, it is just another part of this fantastic journey that you are on.

You might sometimes feel burdened by your empathic abilities, but this is just another part of the process of spiritual awakening. When you are an empath, you can understand the feelings and experiences of other people even if you have never personally felt the same feelings or experienced the same experiences. During your spiritual awakening, you will find that your empathy and your emotions are quite sensitive, and there will be some excellent reasons for these feelings.

You might feel that something important has changed inside of you. You might think that something is different, but you can't explain the feeling. You feel like you want to become someone new who has nothing to do with who you were before. You will visualize things in a wholly unique manner because you are looking at the world with a new vision.

You will know that your old life was not desirable, that something in that life was just not right. You understand that the older adult you used to be was lacking in something meaningful. You finally understand all of the things that you used to do in your life but don't want to anymore and all the old patterns you don't want to repeat. Because you are ready for notable changes in your life, you never want to go back to that old life.

You will want to surround yourself with people who feel like you feel now. Not everyone will evolve in their spiritual process at the same rate, and you might find that you will need to leave some people behind as you grow beyond them. This can be a painful experience, but you need to align yourself with the people who are more like the new you. You need to be with people who have a comparable level of energy and enlightenment. You find it easy to connect with them because you are on the same wavelength they are. You are no longer connecting to people on the superficial level of exchanging ideas, but you are now connecting to others with your soul. This kind of connection is not likely to be ruled by your ego.

You are no longer interested in anything superficial. You are seeking the real thing, those things that are authentic in life. You might be feeling that you have become antisocial or complicated, but you also know that it is not healthy if you are easily able to accept things that are less than perfect. Follow the call of your heart, because it will take you where you should be. It is never easy to experience a spiritual awakening. As you become less entranced in your ego and more aware of the world around you, then you will also become acutely aware of the sadness and despair in the world around you. When you see the suffering in the world and understand the disparity more, it can lead you into depression because you can now feel their pain even if you have never experienced their lifestyles. You will also know that attending to your own needs is no longer enough. You will have a deep need to help other people and make a positive impact on the world around you. You feel that your life will only have meaning when you are helping other people. You will feel incredibly happy even if you have only touched one person. You will feel like your journey here has not been in vain. And many of the activities you used to love will no longer hold any special meaning to you. You have a new purpose in life and new goals. You need to contribute something to the good of the world around you.

Questioning the Status Quo

When you begin to have a greater connection to your true self, you will start to look for answers for your purpose in life and even your very existence. You might begin to question all of the ideas you once took for granted. You might change your focus from the pursuit of money or other forms of instant gratification to looking for experiences that have depth and meaning. Your perspectives will alter, and you will look for purpose in all things. This journey can lead you into painful dark places even while you begin to feel liberated from the person you used to be. The problem with this part of your journey is that you will not be able to truly heal until you can acknowledge the source of what has wounded you in the past. As you begin to awaken, you will make the connection between your current behaviors and your past experiences. You can't indeed become enlightened unless you are willing and able to confront the darkness in your life and consciously acknowledge it.

Diving into your inner psyche to confront your shadows and demons can be difficult to do, but you will need to if you want to continue to grow and develop. You need to know where you came from to be able to understand where you are at this moment in time. When you can do this, you will be able to step into the future and find the self you were meant to be. When you begin to awaken to your true nature, your ego will face certain death, and it will attempt to do everything in its power to keep things as they are, to maintain the status quo. Your ego is the false self that you created with your mind. It does not truly reflect the person you are, the person that is emerging during your transformation. Your ego will cause you to try to revert to your previous behaviors. When your spiritual practice leaves you suffering, you might feel more attached to your old self. But you need to question the status quo and let your ego die so that you can achieve real awakening.

While you are in the process of Kundalini awakening, you will form new perceptions that will be entirely different than your current view of the world. You will feel a lot of doubt, and at times you might doubt your sanity. You will reveal some new things about yourself that will be in direct contradiction to those things that you have always believed. As you get deeper into your Kundalini awakening, you will more closely align with your higher truth. You will begin to attract energies from the Universe that will help you create your new reality. These energies will help light the way for you when the journey becomes too dark for you to want to continue.

Your status quo believes the things you have always considered simply because you have no reason not to accept them. You find yourself complying with the old way of doing things. You follow your beliefs because you have always believed them. When you begin your Kundalini awakening, you will be forced to question the status quo. Questioning is the only way you will be able to grow spiritually. You will not achieve your full transformation until you question the reality of now so that you can move on to the new self that you will become.

Streamlining Your Life

Making your life less cluttered and more streamlined does not just apply to physical clutter, although that is an essential part of streamlining. When you have experienced your Kundalini awakening, you will no longer feel the need to surround yourself with things that have little or no meaning for you. You will need to take some time to look at the objects that fill up your home and question whether or not you need everything that you see. If you are holding onto something that you no longer use, something that gives you no pleasure, then get rid of it. Your house is probably full of things that you don't even recall why you have them, so get rid of them. After the transformation, you will naturally desire a simpler, less cluttered life, and this will begin with your physical possessions.

An even more massive drain on your energy is mental clutter. There are three main areas in which mental clutter will manifest itself in your life, and those are busyness, aspirations, and the overload of information. Part of your mental clutter might be tied up in your physical mess, in the form of books and magazines you mean to read one day, movies you have never watched, and that pile of recipes you have never tried making. One rule that cleaning experts use is the six-month rule: if you haven't used it in six months, then you don't need it. Get rid of it. Unfulfilled aspirations are another area of mental clutter that you will no longer have time or energy for after your kundalini awakening. Think of all of the good intentions you have that you have never gotten around to starting. Then look at them and decide if you still want to do all of these things. Your Kundalini awakening will take you to a place where you will demand simplicity and order, and there might be things on that list that no longer hold any meaning or interest for you. And you should try to reduce the control that social media has over your life, as much as you possibly can.

The worst kind of clutter is the emotional clutter that is present in your life. After your Kundalini awakening, you will find you no longer desire to spend your time on meaningless social obligations. You will no longer do things just because you feel obligated to do them. You will also no longer worry about being forgotten or neglected if you don't take part in every social obligation, as you did before. You will want to create new expectations for yourself and new patterns of behavior. You should never attend a social commitment just because of your feelings that you should. After your transformation, you will only want to do the things that are beneficial for you, and this will let you live a more streamlined and peaceful life.

When you have undergone your Kundalini awakening, and you are free of physical, emotional, and mental clutter. You will no longer waste precious time trying to manage things, people, and situations that should not be an issue in the first place. You will feel lighter and happier. You will suddenly find that you have more time for the things you want to do and the people that you want to see. And you will be loaded with an abundance of energy that will help you reach all of your goals and see your desires through to completion.

Connection with the Divine

There are many names for the Divine energy that is the Kundalini. The Great Goddess or the Divine Feminine is also known as Shakti, the spiritual guide that desires to lead you to reach your very own spiritual pinnacle, your own Nirvana. All people are the vessels of this force of life, no matter their background or culture or anything other designation that might define them; the Divine is in everyone. Even more than energy alone, Shakti is also the location of wisdom, mind, and strength. When you decide to awaken your Kundalini and take the path that will lead you to the force of Shakti, then you will be arousing your calling to the Divine.

What she is will be found within you, and you are what she is. She is just waiting to be awakened from her coiled state at the base of your spine, which she will be able to do when your Kundalini begins to rise through the central channel. She will travel through all of the pathways in your body to help you break through your blockages and clear out all the negativity in your body. Her ultimate goal is to drive you straight to oneness with the Divine. Connecting to your unique essence will serve to awaken your Kundalini as Shakti rises within you ultimately.

Once you have awakened your Kundalini and Shakti has risen to consciousness within you, it will be time for you to connect with your Divine Self. Doing this will provide you with harmony, peace, guidance, and an illuminating light that will come to you through the higher knowledge you will receive. It will now be much easier to turn away from the temptations of the physical world and turn your attention to the power, love, and light of your eternal Self. This will help to reveal the attachments, desires, and illusions that are keeping you held to a lower path because you are on a lower vibrational frequency. The transformation will allow you to find your higher way that will take you to your true enlightenment. You will also more easily recognize those things that are disharmonious, restricting, and limiting the flow of positive energy through your subtle body.

The Divine is always looking for ways to reach you so that He can send you wisdom, love, illumination, and the power to draw higher situations, feelings, and thoughts into your life. The Divine is a wise entity that is ready to show you a better and more joyful way to live. Because of all the good things that are waiting for you, it will not be hard for your subtle body to connect with the Divine. You will only need to set your intentions to connect with the Divine and your own Divine Self. Then you will be open to all of the gifts of consciousness that are awaiting you as you make contact.

Begin by setting your intention to connect with the Divine and to be genuinely open to the inspiration, love, and energy that is waiting for you. During this part of the process, you need to be still and silent. Connecting with the Divine goes far beyond the boundaries of your mind, so you will need to be somewhere that is as free of distractions as possible. Your full powers of receptivity are required to be able to connect with the Divine. So release any random thoughts you might be having. Imagine that you hold all-knowing wisdom, unconditional love, and infinite intelligence. Let your mind be still. Turn your concentration from the outside world to the power that is within you, because that is where you will find the Divine.

Try asking for something from the Divine, some sort of insight or guidance. The Divine will impart the most extensive parts of love, power, and wisdom when you are quiet and peaceful because this is when you are the most receptive. After spending some amount of time in silence, notice how your thoughts have changed. Notice the new feelings you have that are centered on abundance, wisdom, and spiritual visions. You might even receive a message internally that sounds as though it is coming from you, but it is the Divine working through. Do not get discouraged if you don't hear or feel any messages at first, because it may take time to make contact with the Divine fully. Connection with the Divine comes in many different forms. It might be in your deeper breath, an inner knowing, an answer to a question, or a fantastic rush of energy if you do not feel any kind of response that is perfectly fine because your intention to make contact with the Divine is also a form of connection. Some new inspiration or insight may have been given to you, and it will be revealed to you when your time is right for it.

Humans are intended to show the power of the Divine and connect with the Divine. Once you have awakened your Kundalini and complete your transformation, then you will be that much closer to reaching the Divine and your self-realization.

CHAPTER 5
Your Metamorphosis In Four Stages

You will encounter a period during the Kundalini awakening that is often described as being the darkest night of your soul. It is that time when you are at your lowest, just before the transformation to self-realization begins. During this time, you will most likely endure moments of deep despair, times when you feel intense fear, and you will probably wonder why you thought this would be a good idea. Most of these feelings will come from your personality because they are the result of you finally dealing with and identifying with your character.

Because you identify with your thoughts, your personality will be the main focus of your mind's eye. When you speak your opinions and believe that they are correct, you are identifying with your thinking. The story that you are telling will make you feel energetically alive. When you are awakening your Kundalini, your thoughts will turn dark, and this will create a dark vibration in your soul and your body. Once the dark vibration has taken hold, it will continue to send little waves of dark thoughts throughout your mind and body. At this point, you will be temporarily hooked to the dark vibrations, and your soul will be trapped in the circle of reactions between the dark that exists and the light you are seeking.

Your Kundalini will rise because you want it to. You have a spiritual yearning for something better than you have now. The part of yourself that wants to know yourself entirely is the part that will call the Kundalini to rise and take action within you. The method that you use to awaken your Kundalini is not the critical part, because the ultimate result will be the same no matter how the Kundalini is awakened. The energy will push through the blockages in your chakras as it seeks to fill and conquer the central channel and rise to the Crown Chakra.

It is relatively easy to compare the Kundalini awakening to that of a flowing river that has been flooded by heavy rains. As the river becomes saturated, the water will begin to flow through places where it has never gone before. It will creep out into new territory, rearranging the land on its quest to conquer a new area. The same thing will happen to your subtle body when you begin to awaken your Kundalini. The flow might be small at first and difficult for you to notice, but it will eventually grow and develop into a mighty flood that will encompass your entire body, mind, and soul. Because your spirit, body, and mind all intersect in your subtle body, you will be able to experience the results of your awakening on any or all of these levels.

The process as a whole will be different for everyone who undergoes a Kundalini awakening, but several major stages in the awakening process are familiar to everyone. It might take you weeks, or months, or maybe even years (at the longest) to experience some of these stages. The amount of time that passes will depend on how intense a particular Kundalini shift is inside of you. If you feel that you have many changes throughout your lifetime, it might be that you are experiencing one long growth with many smaller cycles throughout your life. The possibilities for how a Kundalini awakening will play out within you are infinite; the number is as endless as the vast number of people who desire to undergo a Kundalini awakening. The process is unique to the individual. The purpose of any guide into this transformation is to give you some guidelines to follow that can help you to progress on your path correctly. It will help you to process the changes and be able to integrate your Kundalini shifts into your progress.

The first stage you will experience in your awakening is often referred to as the burst and bliss stage. Bliss, a feeling of overwhelming happiness, is one of the most intense byproducts of Kundalini awakening. It will feel much like a light in liquid form as it flows through your body in powerful, but gentle, waves that crash and subside. This feeling might happen while you are meditating, or it might happen spontaneously sometime during your day, even though it is a wonderfully ecstatic experience, which should not be the main focus of the experience. While you should enjoy the blissful feeling when you have them, you should not try to stay with them or to recreate them when they are not happening naturally. Let them run their course so that you do not get stuck in one spot of your transformation. The feelings of bliss are the means to the end, not the end themselves.

Kundalini energy shifts might also manifest themselves initially through bursts of physical energy. You may have random periods where you feel very restless, and you feel the need to move continuously. You might find yourself swaying or shaking a body part, like swinging your leg or tapping your foot. Your body is merely trying to process the sudden rush of energy that is flowing through it. When your Kundalini begins to shift, it is much like increasing the level of watts to an electrical appliance. Your physical body is the outlet or the circuit board that is receiving the energy, and it will need to learn how to handle the sudden surge of energy. Your best course of action during this time is to find ways to take care of yourself. Eat nutritious foods, exercise when you can, and try to keep yourself well-grounded in reality. You must be able to grow and develop before you can rise to the next level.

In your next stage, you will experience growth spurts. When your Kundalini goes through its different shifts, you might feel just like you used to think like a child when you were growing, and nothing fit the right way. You will begin to feel like nothing in your life provides you any longer. This feeling might seep into one or more areas of your life. You might start to feel stagnated in your career. You might think that you have somehow disconnected from your friends. You may feel that your wardrobe is outdated, and your home furnishings look suddenly shabby. You might even begin to prefer different colors and different foods than you used to. Your life might feel constraining and old to you, where before your experience was entirely satisfactory to you.

Your internal set point has shifted. Your awareness of your life and your base of perception are different than they were before. You are beginning to form the person who will be the new you, and the old you is beginning to ebb away and disappear. At this point in your transformation, you will have two distinct choices for your path. You can embrace the changes you are experiencing and look forward to what lies ahead, or you can try to pick up the pieces of what is left of you and stuff it back into your old reality. The progress of the remainder of the stages in your transformation will be directly affected by the decision you make at this time.

You will find the path in the future very difficult to navigate if you try to go backward in your transformation. If you can embrace the changes that are happening to you, then you will be able to move forward. You will find the ability to develop reasonable goals for your transformation, and then you will be able to achieve those goals using compassion, clarity, and wisdom. When you reach the end of your shift, then you will realize the goal of a beautiful new life, and it will more closely resemble the new person that you are becoming now. Whatever you eventually decide to do, you will need to make your decision with conscious thought. Many of the people who are in this stage of transformation tend to make hasty or rash decisions. There will be very many times when you will need to make a quick decision to determine your next steps, but this is not one of those times. Right now, you need to take time to consider your options and take slow steps toward your eventual change.

After major shifts, you might tend to feel acutely frustrated, and this is also quite normal. Part of this pain and frustration comes from the fact that your spiritual rates of change and your physical rates of change happen quite differently. The material world moves so much more slowly than the spiritual world does, and you might have a mind full of unique ideas that you would like to manifest without the ability to do so. You will need to follow the proper sequences and take all the steps in order as they come.

When the Kundalini awakening begins, and you are going through shifts in your transformation, you might start to feel that you are on a wildly energetic emotional rollercoaster. You begin to be extremely sensitive to the feelings of other people, and you may suffer from extreme mood swings. Sometimes women will feel these changes more acutely than men will. In the male body, the Kundalini rests at the base of the internal chakras, near the Root Chakra. But in women, the Kundalini is sleeping near the second inner chakra, the Sacral Chakra, which is closely linked to the feminine emotional body. Their subtle body also tends to be more sensitive than the subtle body of the male. Women are usually more likely than men to experience strong mood swings and wildly fluctuating emotions.

You are experiencing the effects of two major shifts when you reach this point in your transformation. New energetic and intuitive abilities are most likely being unleashed as your Kundalini begins to move through your body. You may have the ability to suddenly see things that you were not able to see before. You will also be much more aware of the subtleties of energy in your environment and the people around you. As you begin to develop your new skills, they may become genuinely psychic abilities with skills for healing. They may also be overwhelming in the beginning, as you learn to adjust to the rush of new sensitivities. You will find these adjustments much easier to make if you take some extra time to pamper yourself and take care of your personal needs.

The growth you are experiencing might make you feel resistant, as though you don't want to change, and this can contribute to the emotional swings you are having. You can feel an overwhelming rush of old attachments, insecurities, and fear that rise up inside of you. You may think that you are sliding backward on your path as if you have dealt with these feelings before, and they should be gone now. These are often nothing more than the residual bits of the old patterns of emotional response that have been stuffed down into the deepest parts of your subtle body. The flood of the Kundalini coursing through you has brought them floating to the surface, stirring them up so that you can face these old emotions head-on and get rid of them for good. You can work through this stage by practicing meditation, spending time soul searching and self-inquiry, and writing your thoughts and feelings in a journal.

The heart of the shifting process during the Kundalini awakening is often compared to a school for life teachings. Your mind and spirit are looking for the lessons that they feel you need to learn. Your life will settle down into a new pattern after every shift. During this time, you will experience new ideas, or old ideas in a new disguise, that appear in your life demanding to be addressed. You might face some new opposition in your quest to reach a specific goal. You might need to develop some new goals if you decide that the old ones just aren't working for you any longer. You might face new challenges in your relationships, or you might feel the need to seek out new relationships. You may find yourself in life situations that seem foreign to you because your thoughts and feelings have changed, and parts of your subtle body that have not surfaced before are now on display.

The last shift might have stirred up a lot of old emotional baggage, leaving you with an abundance of emotional residue. There will be even more emotions and thoughts kicked up by the challenges you will face during this stage. While this may feel traumatic in the beginning, it will become less and less painful as you go through more shifts in your transformation. As you progress further into your Kundalini awakening, you will find yourself resisting the changes less and less. Your lessons will become happier and gentler as you begin to look forward to your new abilities. You will learn that growing mentally and emotionally does not need to be painful. Usually, it is your resistance to the growth process that makes it hurt so much.

Now you need to remind yourself that you are experiencing exactly what you asked for. You wanted to undergo a Kundalini awakening. You knew the benefits that would come to you by awakening your Kundalini and going through the transformation. You are going through this entire process in the first place because you had an overwhelming longing for a higher spiritual connection and a desire to grow in all matters. Spend some time enjoying this journey you have undertaken. Try not to dwell too much on the pain you might be feeling, but think about the result. You will be able to help yourself through these changes by reminding yourself of the new wisdom and compassion you are feeling. Think of the supercharged connection to the Divine you will soon be enjoying. A new level of liberation and happiness is right in front of you, and you are being given an excellent opportunity to grow and develop.

The final stage of your metamorphosis is the integration process, but you usually will not notice this part as its separate stage. It is not marked by any significant changes, so it is often overlooked. If you take the time to look back at the person you were before, then you will be surprised to see the changes that you have gone through to get here. You have a new energy level and a new perspective on life, and you are more comfortable in your new transition. You are enjoying a new level of understanding and peace in your life now that you have let go of the old emotional residue that was holding you back in your previous life. On some basic fundamental level, you have reached a new level of maturity.

In one way, your Kundalini awakening will never ultimately end. As many times as you try to seek a new level of spiritual maturity, then you will never entirely complete your shifts. You can find yourself deep in the throes of a new cycle as you are completing the one you are currently in. You will have time to regroup and rest when you are in a lull in the activity, enjoying a period of quiet. You can always choose to slow your growth for a while if you need some time to recuperate. Your spiritual desire will let you know when it is ready for another round of awakening and growing.

Some things will remain constant as you are going through your cycles of change and growth. There are distinct phases to every layer of your transformation. When you first become attached to a new layer, then that is your starting point. But since you are continually transforming, you will eventually become dissatisfied with that phase, and you will be miserable. This is your cue to begin the move to the next phase by letting go of this phase. Once you can drop the attachment to the phase you are in, you will begin another spiritual awakening in which a higher self will emerge. The transformation is fueled by the tremendous amount of energy that is released. Spiritual reactions and profound healing will accompany the biological aspect of the transformations. You might have feelings of one or more of the charismatic symptoms that are associated with spiritual transformation. You might experience weight loss, amplified hearing, telepathy, repressed memories, visions, insights, sudden clarity, out of body experiences, tingling in your body, numbness, flashing lights, and strange noises. These symptoms are mostly due to the changes you are experiencing in your nervous system, as well as your body and your mind. In the days following a spiritual awakening, you might feel enormously elated. You will feel awake and more spiritual because of the direct contact with your higher self. You will never be completely able to forget the wisdom and insights that you received during your revelations, and you should not try to forget them. You will be permanently changed by your Kundalini awakening, and that is the ultimate goal. You will look at the world differently because your system of values has changed.

When you go through the different phases, you may find yourself dropping attachments you had to certain things, places, or even people. Your internal healing will continue even when the joy of your new position begins to settle down. You might experience intense emotions, or you may feel pain in various parts of your body. You might have days when you feel completely exhausted. You might have dark thoughts for several days in a row. Your consciousness might become flooded by the memories of your past life, and you may have disturbing dreams. You might not feel very well physically, and you might be regretting your decision, feeling that you have made many large sacrifices and gained very little to nothing for your effort. During your awakening, every part of you is undergoing immense changes, so you will need to be patient with yourself. This is not the time to undertake anything strenuous.

At the end of your Kundalini awakening, you will choose to surrender to your higher self, the new you that is part of your self-realization. In this context, the act of surrender means to divert your energies from your old habits of acknowledging your personality and into your new way of life that is free of any ego. You can use meditation to quiet your inner voice that comes from the mind if it has not entirely transformed. Your new higher self is that part of you that will work to heal you when it is needed. Your spirit must make the first changes in your new self because your body is merely a reflection of your spirit. If you allow your mind to remain in control, then your transformation will never be complete. When you surrender to the Kundalini awakening experience when you accept the changes that have happened, then your higher self will win in the end, and your transformation will be complete.

CHAPTER 6

Life After Kundalini Awakening

Once you make it through the fires of change and emerge on the other side of your Kundalini awakening, then you will have some period of adjustment. You will need to be able to integrate your new life into whatever part of your old life that you are keeping. You will not be ready to rebuild your life immediately after your transformation. You are feeling different realizations and feelings, and you probably are not sure of who you are now.

You will feel an extraordinary intensity of change inside after your awakening. It is impossible to understand if you have not experienced it yourself, so other people might not know what you are experiencing. When you go through a Kundalini awakening, it is something like experiencing an internal fire, and in the first period after the awakening, you need to let the fires burn down. The burning will eventually subside, and you will be able to begin your rebuilding process. You may not have dealt with all of the issues that were dug up during your awakening, and that is okay. You can always revisit these at a later date, as long as you do not allow them to become a part of you once again.

As human beings, you are an amazing and fascinating creature. When you learn to get out of your way, then you will be an amazing person. You will naturally flow towards the things that support you and are meaningful for you. There are many ways in which you will need to grow up all over again after your Kundalini awakening. All people who experience the transformation will walk a different path because the journey is completely personal. You have cleared out space inside of yourself, and you might be content to simply sit back and observe where you are going and what you are doing and saying. You will begin to get an idea of the kind of life that you want to live while you are enjoying this natural state of affairs. Your soul will intuitively want to live the best possible life. Once you have begun the adjustment process, then you can start to take the actions you need to take to begin to move toward your new life.

This process will be completely different than your old methods, where you consciously plotted every move that you would make. You might do some of that while you are figuring things out. The space in your soul after you have cleaned it out in your awakening will embrace anything you introduce to it. Your soul is a curious entity. No ability or possibility will be left out in your search. Everything in the world is now available to you. This will give you the ability to decide how you want to create your new life and what you want to have in it. This method will only work when you are spiritually awakened, so if you have tried this before with poor results, then don't be afraid to try it again. You are not actively seeking to arrange your new life; you are not actively planning anything right now. You are simply living while your higher self decides what direction your new life will go in. Your intellectual, emotional, and physical tendencies are to try to move back into your old way of life with your old patterns of behavior. Those situations will only reveal what your subconscious mind relates to and not what your new natural, curious soul wants to explore.

In your new life, you will try, and you will fail, and this is perfectly normal. You are learning how your divine intelligence is supposed to work. You can't control the process or even predict how it will go because you will need to take action sometimes and allow life to flow on its own sometimes. You will alternate between receiving from life and taking your actions. You will make mistakes, especially in the beginning. You will know times when you will sit back and receive things when you should be acting, and other times when you should wait to receive what you are trying to act. At those times, the new life you are trying to build will feel like it is falling apart. Be patient; everything will work itself out.

Life after a Kundalini awakening might feel a lot like a mid-life crisis. All the things you have previously committed yourself to have been taken away or are being dissolved right before your eyes. Everything in your life is open for review. Your career, your dietary habits, your family connections, your relationships, all of your old addictions and habits, everything you knew before and understood might now be gone, or it won't mean the same to you. If you react with fear and resistance, then your integration process will be stagnated. Your journey is just beginning, and you will need to meet it with discipline and courage.

You might experience various physical symptoms after the awakening. You might feel overwhelmingly energetic. You might have obvious physical symptoms like periods of trembling, an inability to relax, and visual disturbances. Your symptoms might be more emotional, like feelings of despair, depression, or anxiety. The amount of energy that is coursing through your body after the awakening strains your nervous system to the extent of its limits. Some people will experience a steady and slow onset of symptoms, and some people will experience them in a great rush. Do not let yourself obsess over what you are feeling now, but try to find different methods for relaxation and let the process take its course. The channels of energy are now open, and your body will eventually heal itself. Look for ways to treat and heal your entire body, and try not to focus too much on the individual symptoms.

There may be an overwhelming desire to try new things. You might finally be willing to seek out new situations. You might finally be feeling the courage to do so, or the desperation to leave your old life behind and move on to the new one. These feelings can be quite intense. Some people try new diets, change their jobs, or look for new careers, or even leave established relationships. All of these changes are nothing more than an attempt to deal with the new energy inside of you. And while you are willing to try new experiences, you will be available to receive new kinds of support from unexpected sources. You will eventually meet the right kind of people, you will find the right kinds of classes to take, and you will learn the new skills that you need for your new life. When new things are meant to happen in your life, they will.

When you begin to make the changes you want to make in your new life, you might find that you are more sensitive to some things that you used to tolerate simply. You will need to be more cautious about the things you bring into your life. You might need to spend less time on social media. You might need to begin a new exercise program or experiment with some dietary changes. Listen to your body, because it will let you know what it needs to be whole and healthy. As your nervous system continues to adjust and change, in its drive to accept the new levels of energy that are coursing through it, you will be even more sensitive than you were before. This is a clear sign of future potential and increased awareness, and it is not a sign of weakness.

You will also find that you are more aware of what is happening around you, and you will be more sensitive to the environment that you are in. You will develop a deeper relationship with your soul, and you will pay much more attention to your intuition. You begin to rely more on your inner compass so that the opinions of others no longer mean to you what they used to mean to you. You will become aware that your body needs some special attention and that your chakras might need unique tuning. You will naturally react when you don't feel grounded or comfortable within your skin. You will know what you need better than anyone else will, so you will become your own best healer. This might include a daily practice of meditation or yoga or some other form of exercise. You need to spend some quality time every day with your deeper self, taking time to look beyond your ego and your personality. You will need to use whatever tools you have to allow yourself to evolve and heal.

When you originally become more aware of your new self, you will also be more aware of the part that you play in the workings of the larger world around you. You will develop a heightened sense of compassion for other people as you learn to love yourself more. Your heart is now opened to the sufferings of other people. This will give you the desire to help other people, especially those who are going through their own awakening process. You have an inner knowing of the connection you have with the rest of the world. You will also begin to feel a deeper connection to nature, now that you feel more comfortable in your own body. You will want to care for others while you are caring for yourself.

And you will have an immensely growing sense of purpose in life that will begin to influence you in ways you never thought possible. This is your real destiny. You will be ready to deliver your destiny when you have made the connection to your soul and your heart, when you can channel your energy in positive ways, and when you can get beyond the traumas of your past to be able to heal yourself. You will now know your connection to the Divine, and you can freely express yourself. You will fulfill your destiny by elevating yourself when you can give freely of yourself from your heart. You will work to make the world a better place, and you have a renewed spirit of energy and purpose. You will have realized the true purpose of a Kundalini awakening, and that is the ability to live honestly in your mind and spirit.

CHAPTER 7

Methods For Awakening The Kundalini

If you can sit quietly, closing your eyes, and breathing deeply, you will probably be able to feel your pulse. If you are still, you might be able to feel the energy buzzing around in your body. That is your Kundalini, looking for an outlet. This deeply revered and universally acknowledged energy that pervades your everyday life is waiting for you to unlock it and let it flow. Your Kundalini is an energy that rests at the bottom of your spine like a small coiled serpent. When you release this energy, it will flow freely upward through your chakras to give you an expanding state of your consciousness and a deeper connection with the Divine. This is what is known as a Kundalini awakening.

When you awaken your Kundalini, you will be more balanced spiritually and emotionally as well as being more inspired and creative. The energy of the Kundalini supports your spirit and drives all of the everyday functions of your mind and your body. This awakening has been practiced in India for thousands of years and was brought to the western world as a form of yoga practice. The practice of yoga was originally taught to people as a way to find true spiritual enlightenment. Modern yoga is more concerned with poses, but true Kundalini yoga will help you in your quest for true spiritual enlightenment. Kundalini yoga wants to incorporate the focus on all parts of the person into one holistic practice. This means that energy release is taught for the spirit, mind, and body all at the same time. The physical poses will focus on the key points of energy in the body that will activate the areas that need assistance to allow the energy to flow freely. Specific techniques for breathing will help you to unlock your inner energy and learn to control your breathing. The physical part of the Kundalini yoga practice will help you to achieve a heightened sense of awareness.

Kundalini meditation will help you awake your higher consciousness and the energy of the Kundalini. While you are meditating, it is important to breathe properly to attain peace. Practice breathing directly into your tailbone, since this is where the Kundalini is coiled and waiting for its awakening. While you are breathing, try to direct the breath you are taking down through your spine and then back up, all the way to the top of your head. Focus continually on the upward movement of your breath. Then let the breath cycle down to your heart, and then back up. Complete your cycles of breathing with some sort of mantra or chant while you are focusing on the breath.

Kundalini Yoga

Since your body is a complex system that holds vast systems of energy, it will need specific methods of yoga for energizing it. Kundalini yoga was developed centuries ago for the specific purpose of awakening the Kundalini by opening the seven internal chakras.

Unlock the Root Chakra with the Crow Pose. Stand straight and tall with your feet close together and your arms stretched out in front of you, palms facing down. Slowly drop to a deep squat, with your bottom almost resting on the floor. Hold it for five seconds and then slowly come back to a standing position. Keep holding your arms straight out in front of you the entire time.

Unlock your Sacral Chakra with the Frog Pose. Leave your toes planted tightly on the ground and lift your heels, keeping them close together. Set your hands on the ground in front of you and look forward. Inhale deeply through your nose and then straighten your knees while you drop your head toward the ground. Then let out your exhale as you drop back into the squat.

Unlock your Solar Plexus Chakra with the Stretch Pose. Lie on your back on the ground or a yoga mat. Lift your feet about six or seven inches off of the ground and lift your head off the ground. Bring your arms up beside your body so that they are in the air just above the level of your hips. Breathe deeply and slowly.

Unlock your Heart Chakra with the Camel Pose. This pose needs to be done carefully so that you do not strain your lower back. Kneel down on the floor, with your leg from your knee to your feet on the floor. The top part of your feet will be resting flat on the floor. Bend backward slowly and grab your ankles with your hands, allowing your head to drop back and down as far as possible. If you are not able to stretch that far back, then place the palms of your hands on your hips near the small of your back and stretch back only as far as you feel comfortable doing.

Unlock your Throat Chakra with the Cobra Pose. Lie on your stomach on the ground. Put your hands flat on the floor right under your shoulders, with your palms lying flat on the floor. Push straight up with your arms, lifting your heart and letting your head follow, but keep your pelvic area on the floor. If stretching this far is too much for you, just come up part of the way.

Unlock your Third Eye Chakra with the Guru Pranam Pose. Kneel down on the floor with the top part of your feet on the floor, and sit back on your heels with your spine straight. Bring your torso down over your thighs and let your forehead rest on the ground. Lay your arms on the ground in front of you, so that they are extended flat in front of you.

Unlock your Crown Chakra with the Sat Kriya Pose. Sit back on your heels and stretch your arms straight up over your head, with your fingers pointing straight up. Let your elbows hug your ears. While you hold this position, chant the words 'sat nam' over and over; slowly and carefully. Keep your eyes closed. This particular yoga pose will work to open up all of your chakras. It will specifically work to wake up the energy of your Kundalini and help it to work upward along your spine and through your chakras.

Keep in mind that there is no best pose, and no one chakra will stand on its own without the others. The entire chakra system works together in an interrelated and holistic system. You can't work on just one of the chakras and ignore the needs of the others. Your Lower Triangle of chakras, the lower three, deal with things that need to be eliminated from your body. The Upper Triangle of the upper three chakras focuses on the accumulation of energy in the body. The two triangles meet in the middle of the body at the Heart Chakra, which works to balance the forces between the chakras.

Kundalini Meditation

While the exact origins of Kundalini meditation are not known, the traditions date back to about three thousand years ago. The word Kundalini translates to a coiled snake. This refers to the belief that everyone has divine energy that they carry coiled up at the base of their spine. The practice of Kundalini meditation works to awaken the coiled snake, release it, and harness the energy for the good of the human. Besides awakening, the Kundalini, practicing this form of meditation will also promote greater mindfulness, relieve stress, and help you to become more mindful and aware of your body and its place in the world.

The most important purpose of the meditation is to move the energy of the Kundalini through your body. The concept states that the energy that is coiled at the base of your spine will need to be released to travel through your seven internal chakras. Releasing this energy will create a communication system between your body and your mind. This communication will work to relieve your spiritual, mental, and physical issues. Bringing awareness to all parts of your body by getting you connected with your breath is meant to help you to be more present in your current time and space, help you establish a smooth new rhythm, and assist you in communicating with the higher version of yourself.

Kundalini meditation is not a system of beliefs. It is a practice that you will do daily to cleanse your spiritual body and your mind. It will help you counteract physical tiredness and manage the stress of daily life. It will also work to calm your mind and balance your chakras so that you are no longer simply reacting to the stimulus in your environment, but you are acting with purpose in your life.

Follow the steps of Kundalini meditation carefully. Start with a basic form of meditation and work to a deeper and longer meditation once you have mastered that form. This is not a race or a goal but a practice. Since it is better, to begin with a small routine, pick a time length that is manageable in your current schedule. You can always adjust later. You will feel overwhelmed if you try to do too much too quickly, and this could sabotage your efforts. You can do just five or ten minutes each day, and you will receive benefits from it.

Choose the location for your meditation. While you can do your meditation anywhere, you will want to be in a spot that is quiet and free from distractions. This should be somewhere that is peaceful and relaxing for you. If you can set aside a regular spot, then you might want to put some of your most favorite things there. Dress in clothes that feel comfortable for you. Since everyone has their idea of what is comfortable, there are no special outfits that you will need to have. Many people who practice meditation prefer to do it in some flowing, loose garment that is soft to the touch. You will need to feel comfortable so that you will be able to get into your practice easily. You might want to drape a soft cloth over your head to enhance the feeling you are trying to create.

Many people like to practice early in the morning to get a good start to their day. Others say practicing at night, just before going to bed, helps them to relax and sleep deeply. This is also left up to your personal preference. Since your body will be busy digesting your food, it is not recommended that you meditate directly after eating. Where you sit during meditation is also your choice. You can sit on the floor with your legs crossed, as it is often a picture, or you can sit in a comfortable chair. Not everyone is able to sit down on the floor and get back up with ease! The main point in where and how you choose to sit is that you need to sit somewhere that your spine will be straight and upright.

Your practice can last anywhere from five minutes to three hours. Again, this is also determined by you and your needs and your schedule. Maybe you can do a short meditation before beginning your day, and then a longer one just before bed to help you relax. There is no one correct answer. You will need to choose your mantra. This is the saying that you will repeat, out loud or in your mind, to help you focus during your meditation. The mantra should be something that you will feel comfortable saying. Its purpose is to direct your focus and your energy during meditation. Once you become comfortable with your mantra, you may want to think it to yourself at various times when you feel stressed, as a way to help you calm down. The main point of your mantra, besides helping you focus, is to help you break out of your old patterns. It needs to reflect the state that you want to be in, not the state that you are in.

Focus on your breath and let it slow down gradually. Your goal is for each round of breathing, and inhale and an exhale, to least about eight or nine seconds. Always breathe through your nose. While you are practicing your breathing, focus on how the air is moving through your body, and helping you to relax. If your thoughts begin to wander, just bring them back to the present by focusing more on your mantra and your breathing. Have a timer already set so that you are not watching the clock while you meditate, if you are on a time schedule. Complete your session of meditation by taking a deeper breath as you slowly raise your arms above your head, to release any final toxins that might be lingering in your body. Then exhale and relax.

Increase the length of the time that you meditate gradually as your schedule allows. Watch for the energy moving along your spine as you focus on your breathing. Even if you can only manage two minutes of meditation at first, then you are doing just fine. You will need some amount of practice to be able to clear your mind and focus on your breathing, especially if you are highly stressed in your daily life. Eventually, you will find it easy to enter the state of meditation, and then this will work its way over into other areas of your life. You will find that you are not so reactive during the day, and that little annoyances don't annoy or aggravate you the way they used to.

Chanting

Chanting can be an easy yet powerful way to awaken the Kundalini inside of you. Chanting is often referred to as a practice of yoga for your mind. When you are chanting a mantra, you are trying to reach one of three levels of consciousness. If you speak the chant out loud, then you are trying to activate the physical level of your being. When you whisper the mantra in your chanting, you are looking for love, someone to belong to, and inner peace. When mantras are thought and not spoken, they are guided toward the divine in you and the other worlds. Do things that you can do to make your mantra more powerful for you. One of these is to visualize the mantra being written while you are saying or thinking it. The other method is to listen to the word actively while you are saying it.

The purpose of chanting, especially when it is done as a part of meditation, is to close out the outside world and have a few minutes of peace with you. Choose your mantra carefully because you should know the meaning of the word, and it should mean something to you. Try one of these mantras that are used for chanting

- Ohm is probably the one mantra that comes to people's minds when they think of chanting. This word means that it is, it will be, or it will become. Its specific sound makes it the sound of the universe. The word itself represents the cycle of life and death and reincarnation.

- Satchitananda, or Sat Chit Ananda, is a compound word in the Sanskrit language. Sat means being present or being alive. Chit means to acknowledge, feel, or comprehend. Ananda means happiness, joy, or bliss. So when it is said all together, it means that the chanter is present in the feeling of joy, or another comparable phrase.

- Aham-Prema will help you bring together your soul, mind, and body in a feeling of great peace. It helps clear distractions from your mind and leaves your past in the past. It means I am Divine love.

You can also write your mantra for chanting, as many people like to do. This will make it specific to you and what you need in your life. Think of a few things that you are craving mentally or spiritually right now. It might be love, peace, forgiveness, or one of many other things. The mantra needs to be said in a positive tone. You would not say 'I am not afraid,' but you would say 'I am strong and brave.' While this might feel strange to you at first, relax and give it time to develop. Chanting a mantra, just like yoga or meditation, are practice and not a goal.

Teacher of Kundalini

Some people who will assert that you should never try to awaken your Kundalini on your own because it is too dangerous, that you should always have the assistance of a trained teacher to guide you along your path. If you feel that you will need to have someone like this in your life, it is your personal preference, but it is not really needed.

There is nothing dangerous about awakening your Kundalini. The danger that many people see is the opening up of old wounds and old traumas that might cause a strong negative reaction within you. You will not be able to rise to full enlightenment until you are able to let go of the past. Simply acknowledging a past trauma will not be enough. You will need to examine it for what it was, acknowledge the effect it has had on your life, and then be strong enough to let it go. Many people hold onto old wounds as some sort of security blanket. As long as this problem is with them, then they will not need to function above a specific level in life. Kundalini gives you the possibility of living a pure, high-functioning life, but to do that, you must purge your soul of all of the old darkness so that you can step out and walk in the light of the Divine.

So if you feel you need a teacher for your Kundalini awakening, look for one who has been helping people successfully and is willing to work on your schedule and at your pace. Some people move easily into enlightenment, and other people take longer. You will need to deal with the darkness as it comes, and you will need to do this at your own pace. But when you have achieved full Kundalini awakening, when you have cast off your old life and stepped into the light of the new day, you will feel completely fulfilled.

CONCLUSION

Thank you for making it through to the end of *Kundalini and the Chakras*; let's hope it was informative and that it was able to provide you with all of the tools you need to achieve your goals whatever they may be.

The next step is to take the information that you learned by reading this book and apply it to your own life. If there is any part of your personal life that is not measuring up to the way you expected it to be, then that might be a sign that you need a Kundalini awakening. Just the mere fact that you were curious enough about it to read this book means that you are seeking something more in your life, and Kundalini awakening is just the thing that you need.

Use the information that you have read to begin working on yourself and your own transformation. Remember that the way will now always be smooth, and you will need to be prepared to deal with things you feel are better left alone, but in the end your mind and your spirit will be filled with a kind of peace that you have never known in your life. A Kundalini awakening will provide you with this peace and the energy to maintain your glorious new life.

Finally, if you found this book useful in any way, a review on Amazon is always appreciated!

DESCRIPTION

Do you constantly feel as though there is something important missing in your life? Is your life a constant cycle of disappointments and missed opportunities? Do you struggle to lose weight or find enough energy to make it through to the end of the day? Did you always feel that life needed to be something more than just maintaining a routine, that there was something much better out there, if you could just find it? If any of this sounds like you, then you are holding the book in your hands that will turn your life around.

Kundalini Awakening is the book that you need right now to improve your life and get out of that horribly boring rut you are stuck in. You are probably blocked internally, mentally, emotionally, and spiritually. Awakening your Kundalini will help you with all of that and more.

Your Kundalini energy is a small area at the base of your spine that has been with you since you were born, and it will be with you until the day you leave this world. You have carried it with you all of the time but you probably don't know what it can do for you, or else you would not be stuck in this rut. But when you awaken your Kundalini you will experience many marvelous benefits like

- Increased energy
- Clear thoughts
- Happy mind
- Peaceful soul

If all of this sounds impossible to achieve, don't worry. You will get all of this and more when you awaken your Kundalini and experience your own spiritual transformation. The energy of the Kundalini will cycle through your physical body and enable you to finally accomplish all of the things you have ever wanted to do. It can make you

- More productive
- More mindful
- More caring

- More divine thinking

You will soon know just how easy it is for you to tap into the powers in your own mind and soul. Your spirit will receive an intense cleansing, guaranteed to eliminate all of the worldly garbage you have built up over the years. Your conscious mind will finally be free to think clearly and effortlessly, and your physical body will reap all the rewards of all of these improvements.

But you won't really know all of the great things that are waiting for you until you take this book home and get started on your own Kundalini awakening. These steps that you will follow, as they are written in this book, will bring you to the spiritual, mental, emotional, and physical level you have always wanted to achieve but did not know how to find. Buy this book now and go home and get started on the journey of a lifetime, the journey that you will take by yourself and for yourself, the journey that will set you free to be the person you have always wanted to be.